D0948908

THE

Mississippi Quarterly

SERIES IN SOUTHERN LITERATURE

THE

Mississippi Quarterly

SERIES IN SOUTHERN LITERATURE

under the general editorship of

PEYTON W. WILLIAMS

THE FORM DISCOVERED

Essays on the Achievement of Andrew Lytle

M. E. BRADFORD, EDITOR

A FAULKNER MISCELLANY

JAMES B. MERIWETHER, EDITOR

A FAULKNER MISCELLANY

World War II Monument, Oxford, Mississippi

A
FAULKNER
MISCELLANY

EDITED BY
JAMES B. MERIWETHER

PUBLISHED FOR THE *MISSISSIPPI QUARTERLY* BY THE
UNIVERSITY PRESS OF MISSISSIPPI
JACKSON

The essays by Noel Polk, Thomas L. Mc-
Haney, Keen Butterworth, Michael Millgate,
and Eileen Gregory appeared previously in
the *Mississippi Quarterly*, 26, (Summer 1973).

THIS VOLUME IS AUTHORIZED
AND SPONSORED BY
MISSISSIPPI STATE UNIVERSITY
MISSISSIPPI STATE, MISSISSIPPI

CONTENTS

The
Mississippi Quarterly
Series
in Southern Literature

Mississippi Quarterly: The Journal of Southern Culture, as its title implies, is an interdisciplinary journal dealing with all aspects of the life and civilization of the American South; it is now in its twenty-sixth year of publication under the sponsorship of Mississippi State University. For many years, and with increasing distinction, the *Quarterly* has given major attention to Southern writers of all periods by publishing critical and scholarly articles, bibliographies, edited source materials, letters and reviews; by sponsoring symposia; and by publishing numerous special issues each concerned with the work of a single Southern author. This year, in conjunction with Mississippi State University and the University Press of Mississippi, it is initiating a series of volumes to be designated The *Mississippi Quarterly* Series in Southern Literature. The plan includes a general series, of which *The Form Discovered: Essays on the Achievement of Andrew Lytle* has already appeared; a sub-series on William Faulkner, of which *A Faulkner Miscellany* is the first volume; and a second sub-series of bibliographical studies. The general series is intended to include editions of significant source materials for the study of Southern letters as well as further general critical and scholarly works.

Editor's Foreword

This collection is a revision of the Summer, 1973 issue of the *Mississippi Quarterly* (volume XXVI, no. 3), which was the tenth in the annual series of Faulkner issues of that journal that I have edited. The book reviews and two short essays were dropped from that issue. For this book, additions and corrections to the pieces by Professors Butterworth and Millgate were made; and the illustrations, the essays by Fr. Samway and myself, and the two versions of Faulkner's 1961 Caracas speech have been added.

Like the *Mississippi Quarterly* issue upon which it is based, *A Faulkner Miscellany* concerns itself with what is one of the most significant, but one of the least studied, areas of the Faulkner field: his manuscripts and typescripts, his unpublished and uncollected writings. It was made possible by the great generosity of Mrs. Jill Faulkner Summers, Faulkner's daughter and literary executrix. Very grateful thanks are rendered her for approving the publication of the Faulkner writings which appear here for the first time, and for permitting access to and quotation from the many Faulkner manuscripts and typescripts upon which the other pieces in this volume depend. Especial thanks are due Mrs. Summers for making available to me the "Rowan Oak" papers, that group of his manuscripts and typescripts which turned up in August 1970 in a closet in Faulkner's house in Oxford. Those papers are, at the time of the writing of this preface, still in a vault at the University of Mississippi, and by Mrs. Summers' wishes are closed to further investigation. But she very kindly arranged for photocopies to be made available to me in order to carry out certain bibliographical and editorial tasks which she had entrusted to me (as she had previously done for Professor Joseph Blotner in order to enable him to incorporate information from them into his biography of Faulkner). I should also like to thank Professor James W. Webb for assistance in my work on these papers. Professor Blotner very kindly made avail-

able the translation by Muna Lee of the Caracas speech, which
had been given him by Miss Lee.

Thanks are also due to Dr. F. Warren Roberts, director of the
Humanities Research Center at the University of Texas, and to
Dr. Lola Szladits, curator of the Berg Collection, New York
Public Library, for their cooperation and assistance.

And finally, very grateful acknowledgment is due Dr. John
K. Bettersworth, founding editor of the *Mississippi Quarterly*
and Vice-President for Academic Affairs of Mississippi State
University, and Professor Peyton Williams, editor of the *Quarterly,* for their advice and support, which have been essential at
every stage of this project.

JAMES B. MERIWETHER
February, 1974

A FAULKNER MISCELLANY

NOEL POLK

University of Texas at Arlington

William Faulkner's *Marionettes**

ALL OF WILLIAM FAULKNER'S unpublished work, of course, deserves the serious scrutiny it is now beginning to get; but *Marionettes: A Play in One Act,* which he wrote (apparently in 1920), hand-printed, -decorated, and -bound, during his association with the drama group at the University of Mississippi,[1] is of interest to Faulknerians both for the portrait it paints of Faulkner the artist at this very early point in his career, and for the rather special relationship it bears to the rest of his *oeuvre.* Indeed, like the host of poems, published and unpublished, which he wrote during these years, *Marionettes* is, among other things, a remarkable synthesis of his reading up to that time and is therefore a rich mine for source study. But quite apart from its value as a "source," it has a very sophisticated literary identity of its own; and though it is obviously the work of a young man, showy and self-conscious, it is also the work of a very ambitious and self-confident young man, who is fully aware of his gift if not yet of his powers, and who is eager, as it were, to try his wings on something a bit more complex and sustained than short poems. One readily sees in it the same rigid artistic discipline that is evident in the later

---

* I am deeply grateful to Mrs. Jill Faulkner Summers, Faulkner's daughter and literary executrix, for allowing me to quote from the unpublished manuscript copies of *Marionettes,* two of which are at the University of Texas, and from other unpublished manuscripts there. I would also like to thank the Faculty Committee on the Use of Historical and Literary Manuscripts of the University of Texas for permission to examine the Texas Faulkner collection, and Dr. F. Warren Roberts, Dr. David Farmer, and the staff of the Humanities Research Center at Texas for their cordiality and cooperation in expediting my work there.

[1] At least four scholars have drawn attention to *Marionettes:* James B. Meriwether, *The Literary Career of William Faulkner* (Princeton, 1961; reissue, Columbia, S. C., 1971), pp. 8-9; Carvel Collins, "Faulkner at the University of Mississippi" in his edition of *William Faulkner: Early Prose and Poetry* (Boston, 1962), pp. 11-13, 17-18; Michael Millgate, *The Achievement of William Faulkner* (New York, 1966), pp. 8-9; and James E. Kibler, Jr., "William Faulkner and Provincetown Drama, 1920-1922," *Mississippi Quarterly* 22 (Summer 1969), 229, 234-235.

works—it has the tightness of construction and the concentration of effect which characterize the work of the French Symbolist poets, to whom he was going to school—and it flatly predicts many of the techniques, even themes and images, which are so important to his fiction.

The plot of *Marionettes* is very simple—Pierrot seduces Marietta and then abandons her—but Faulkner supports it with a number of complex and sophisticated artistic techniques and devices, most of which he was to use in later work: the frame, the counterpointed plot, and, not surprisingly, diverse viewpoints of the central action. These, interwoven with a number of important symbols, images, and allusions, permit him to treat a number of themes common to his later fiction—Time, Change, frustrated sexuality, sterility and fecundity—and give to *Marionettes* a thematic, if perhaps not quite philosophical, weight, which greatly belies its slight size. *Marionettes* represents, then, an ambitious—perhaps the most ambitious—accomplishment of Faulkner's early career, and as such is of particular significance to any understanding of Faulkner's development as an artist.

According to his own statement some years later, Faulkner printed and bound, by hand, six copies.[2] At least four of these have survived—two at the University of Texas have 51 pages each; one in the possession of a private collector has 55 pages;[3] and Carvel Collins has called attention to one copy with 53 pages[4]—and despite Faulkner's statement that he "signed none of them," three of these copies are indeed signed on the title page, and the fourth bears his signature at the bottom of the final illustration. All four copies appear to have basically the

---

[2] Meriwether, *Literary Career,* p. 9, quotes Faulkner's reply to Raymond Green's query of 9 February 1932: "I wrote a play by that name once. It was never printed. I made and bound 6 copies by hand. I signed none of them. There may also be a mss. It was long ago and I dont remember."

[3] This is the copy which Meriwether describes, *Literary Career,* pp. 8-9.

[4] *Early Prose and Poetry,* p. 18. Barbara Izard and Clara Hieronymus, *Requiem for a Nun: Onstage and Off* (Nashville, 1970), p. 135, saw a third *Marionettes* in the University of Texas collection, a 53-page copy, perhaps the one Collins describes; but it was not listed in the catalog, or otherwise available, when I examined the other two copies in May 1973.

same text, with some stylistic variations, and the same nine illustrations. The two copies at Texas, the only two I have examined in their entirety, are written on standard 8½" x 11" leaves, folded once across the width, and sewn into a single gathering; they are bound in strict black and white, a scheme consistent with the colorless formality and regularity of both illustrations and text.

Michael Millgate has suggested that *Marionettes'* "chief importance" is in this aspect of its production, its "combination of text with related illustrations and . . . its overall stylisation of language, action and line."[5] And though I don't quite agree that this is its "chief" importance—that is, as opposed to the actual content of the play—Faulkner's concern with the physical appearance of the book is very interesting indeed. For *Marionettes* is one of a series of manuscript pamphlets which he wrote, printed, decorated, and bound by hand during the twenties,[6] and the concern is one which extends into at least two of his published works. He was, for example, very interested in the physical make-up of his first book, *The Marble Faun;* Phil Stone wrote to Four Seas Publishers, apparently when returning page proof of the poem, conveying Faulkner's suggestion that he preferred the book bound in pale green boards, with straw-colored labels on the front and on the spine.[7] More interestingly, however, the expertise he gained in designing the format and actually binding this series of pamphlets puts into a slightly altered perspective his irritation, in 1929, with Ben Wasson's editing of *The Sound and the Fury:* his complaint not just that Wasson's unauthorized tampering interfered with the content of the altered passages, but that the printed text, as it stood, presented "a most dull and poorly articulated picture to [his] eye," and his wish that "publishing was advanced enough" for the first section to be printed using different colored inks to indicate time shifts.[8]

---

[5] *Achievement,* p. 8.

[6] See " 'Hong Li' and *Royal Street:* The New Orleans Sketches in Manuscript" in this issue of *Mississippi Quarterly.*

[7] Stone's correspondence with Four Seas in the fall of 1924 is described and quoted from in the Swann Galleries, Inc. auction catalogue for April 25, 1963. These papers are now at the University of Virginia.

[8] Faulkner to Wasson. Quoted in Millgate, *Achievement,* p. 94.

Marionettes is most significant, however, for its purely literary qualities. As I have suggested, it is a very self-conscious display of his reading; and yet the display is, in its way, so deliberate and controlled, not just in the allusions to specific authors, but in the whole evocation of the mood and tone of *fin de siècle* art and morality, that it is in a real sense an organic part of the whole, a frame of reference if not quite a controlling metaphor, rather than mere decoration; and it gives *Marionettes* a direct relationship with both nineteenth-century decadence and the post-World War I Wasteland malaise which informed so much of American literature in the twenties.

Source-hunting is at best, of course, a risky business, and with an author like Faulkner, who was so omnivorous and catholic a reader, the problems are multiplied many times. There are numerous starting points, however, for hunting *Marionettes'* sources, including especially the writers whom Faulkner translates, reviews, or otherwise alludes to in the writing he did for *The Mississippian,* which has been collected in Collins' edition of *Early Prose and Poetry:* Verlaine, Mallarmé, Swinburne, Wilde, Housman, Millay, O'Neill, etcetera.[9] Collins also suggests the influence of Amy Lowell's "Patterns" on *Marionettes,*[10] and Michael Millgate, calling attention to the drawings, believes that the Aubrey Beardsley-illustrated edition of Oscar Wilde's *Salomé,* which was in Faulkner's library at the time of his death, may have been at least one source of inspiration "for the stylisation and vague, *fin de siècle* sensuality of the play itself and for the manner of its 'publication'."[11] The most pervasive influence, however, seems to be that of the

---

[9] Richard P. Adams, in the first chapter, "Apprenticeship," of his *Faulkner: Myth and Motion* (Princeton, 1968), pp. 16-56, and Margaret Yonce, in her fine dissertation, *"Soldiers' Pay*: A Critical Study of William Faulkner's First Novel" (University of South Carolina, 1970), offer particularly useful discussions of influences on Faulkner's early work. See also Cleanth Brooks, "Faulkner as Poet," *Southern Literary Journal* 1 (December 1968), 5-19; Addison C. Bross, *"Soldiers' Pay* and the Art of Aubrey Beardsley," *American Quarterly,* 19 (Spring 1967), 3-23; H. Edward Richardson, "The Decadence in Faulkner's First [sic] Novel. The Faun, the Worm, and the Tower," *Etudes Anglaises,* 21 (July-September 1968), 225-235; and M. Gidley, "One Continuous Force: Notes on Faulkner's Extra-Literary Reading," *Mississippi Quarterly,* 23 (Summer 1970), 299-314.

[10] *Early Prose and Poetry,* p. 18.

[11] *Achievement,* pp. 8-9.

Symbolists: not only Verlaine and Mallarmé, whose specific influence will be discussed later, but a whole host of other writers of late nineteenth-century Europe—Laforgue, Huysmans, Baudelaire, de Gourmont, Valery, Gautier, and Flaubert, to name only a few, whom he seems to have been reading at this time.[12]

I will try to suggest in this essay several sources for particular matters, but it will be useful to discuss here at least one or two of the major borrowings. The most obvious ancestor of *Marionettes* is Verlaine, four of whose poems Faulkner translated or adapted for *The Mississippian*,[13] and two of which, "Fantoches" and "Clair de Lune" are specifically related to the play. "Fantoches," whose title translates "Puppets," has its *commedia dell'arte* characters plotting in the light of the moon, which watches over the proceedings without the slightest involvement in or concern for human affairs—as Faulkner describes it in a line not from the Verlaine poem, but one borrowed, as Richard P. Adams has pointed out,[14] from Jules Laforgue's poem *"Complainte de cette bonne lune,"* perhaps through Eliot's paraphrase in his "Rhapsody on a Windy Night" —*la lune ne garde aucune rancune:* the moon, cold and passionless, bears no grudges against mortals. "Clair de Lune," however, is more directly related, since the situation it describes is, in essence, an outline of the play—the garden where the masquers dance and sing in their vain attempts to hide, from themselves, the essential sadness of their lives, while the moon, again calm, passionless, and eternal, looks on in splendid ironical contrast:

> Your soul is a lovely garden, and go
> There masque and bergamasque charmingly,

---

[12] Collins, for example, *Early Prose and Poetry*, p. 13, says that Faulkner "imported" the French Symbolists to the University of Mississippi campus, and even though for many of the writers just listed I could not find specific indebtedness, the general mood and tone of their works make it evident that Faulkner was reading them—and others—heavily. Readers familiar with nineteenth-century European literature will not need to have my own real limitations in that area pointed out. I am grateful to my colleague Dr. Thomas Ryan for discussing the subject with me and for giving me several valuable suggestions.

[13] Collected in *Early Prose and Poetry*: "Fantoches," p. 57; "Clair de Lune," p. 58; "Streets," p. 59, and "A Clymène," p. 61.

[14] "Apprenticeship," p. 39.

Playing the lute and dancing and also
Sad beneath their disguising [fantasy].[15]

All are singing in a minor key
Of conqueror love and life opportune,
Yet seem to doubt their joyous revelry
As their song melts in the light of the moon.

In the calm moonlight, so lovely fair
That makes the birds dream in the slender trees,
While fountains dream among the statues there;
Slim fountains sob in silver ecstasies.

Finally, in his fine essay on "Faulkner and Provincetown Drama," James E. Kibler, Jr., contends that Edna St. Vincent Millay's *Aria da Capo*, which Faulkner reviewed in *The Mississippian* for 13 January 1922,[16] is also a direct influence on *Marionettes*, and uses his arguments to disprove the 1920 date which Faulkner put on at least three of the copies he made:

The similarities between this play and Faulkner's own *Marionettes* are significant. First, the title *Marionettes: A Play in One Act* parallels *Aria da Capo: A Play in One Act*, and the main character of both is Pierrot. Also, there are other close likeness[es]. Faulkner's hand-lettered title-page and list of characters in the University of Texas copy are spaced exactly as in the New York Kennerley 1921 edition of *Aria*. A comparison of these pages reveals only one minor difference in wording and spacing except of course Faulkner's substitution of his own title, name, and the names of characters other than Pierrot. The lists of characters in both copies are given the same heading and occupy separate pages. Pierrot is the first character listed in each. The costumes in both plays are too similar to be coincidental, as is the scenery—a formal garden with a moon prominent in a silhouetted background. Up front is a long table at which Pierrot sits as the curtain opens. There are many other close parallels in scenery, phrasing, characterization, and action which cannot be directly quoted. But from the similarities here stated, it is clear that Faulkner knew *Aria* before he wrote his play and may have had a printed version of it before him when he hand-lettered this copy of *Marionettes*.

It is unlikely that he saw the play in 1919; and if he was not acquainted with it through *Reedy's Mirror* (March 18, 1920) or *The Chapbook* (August 1920), his own copy of the Kennerley 1921

---

[15] I have adopted Collins' suggestion, *Early Prose and Poetry*, p. 128, that "fantasy," instead of the apparently misprinted "fanchise" is the correct word here.

[16] Reprinted in *Early Prose and Poetry*, pp. 84-85.

edition is presumably the one which he used for the review of January 13, 1922, and is the source by which he knew the play. If this is the case, the 1920 date on the copy of *Marionettes* signed by Wasson is incorrect; and the play would date from late December 1921 or some time thereafter.[17]

Some of the evidence here assembled is interesting, but Kibler's argument, it seems to me, is unconvincing on several counts: A lot of titles have the designation "A Play in One [or Two or Three] Act" appended. Faulkner certainly did not need to have read *Aria* to know the character of Pierrot, a traditional character-type in much of European literature who appears frequently in Verlaine's *Fêtes Galantes,* the volume of poems in which appeared all four of the poems Faulkner translated from Verlaine, and in the poetry of Jules Laforgue; and, in fact, Faulkner had used Pierrot in his poem "Nocturne," published in the 1920-1921 *Ole Miss.*[18] Pierrot's costume, the baggy clown suit, is more or less traditional with the centuries-old *commedia dell'arte* character, as is, in a general way, his essential behavioral pattern; Marietta is hardly the happily sexual Columbine, whom Faulkner had also used in "Nocturne," but another type, as I will suggest, altogether. Finally, I simply am not so struck with the "close parallels" in phrasing which Kibler suggests.

Further, it seems to me demonstrable that Faulkner did know, and use, the printed version of a play by Laurence Housman and H. Granville Barker entitled *Prunella, or Love in a Dutch Garden.*[19] There is no evidence that Faulkner knew it, beyond its numerous parallels with *Marionettes,* and really no way to prove that he could have known it, except to infer from his friendship with drama critic and novelist Stark Young the possibility that Young, or even Phil Stone, could have given it to him to read. But *Prunella* has all of the characteristic similarities with *Marionettes* which Kibler suggests *Aria da Capo* has, and even some specific plot parallels which *Aria* does not have: it is bound, if not quite so elaborately or decoratively, in the same slightly larger than octavo-size form as *Marionettes* and *Aria;* the list of characters, called here

---

[17] Kibler, "Faulkner and Provincetown Drama," pp. 234-235.
[18] *Early Prose and Poetry,* pp. 82-83.
[19] London, 1906.

"Dramatis Personae," however, is headed with the name of Pierrot. The action takes place in a highly formal garden, hedged around by a fence, with a fountain in the middle. Like Marietta, Prunella is the illegitimate child of a mother who had been seduced by a Don Juan type, and then subsequently abandoned. Both Marietta and Prunella, rather like Quentin Compson, some years later, have been brought by their mothers back to the garden, where they have been reared by three maiden aunts: Prunella's are named, appropriately, Prim, Prude, and Privacy; Pierrot identifies Marietta's aunts as "three grey aunts,/Three drab grey moths . . ." (p. [22]) ; and both gardens go to ruin when Marietta and Prunella are taken away. Finally, both Pierrots claim kinship with the moon: Prunella's lover tells her he is the man in the moon, and Marietta's sings that the moon is his "foster mother in the sky." Even though, then, *Prunella* is for the most part a rather fluffy and insubstantial romantic comedy, in which Prunella and Pierrot are happily reunited after their trials, whereas in *Marionettes* they are not, the relationships between the two plays are very real. There seems to me, therefore, no reason to think of *Aria da Capo* as a direct ancestor of *Marionettes;* and no real reason to disbelieve the 1920 date which Faulkner gave it.

*   *   *   *   *

Marionettes opens with a description of the stage setting, which establishes the pervasive tone of formality and artificiality in the play, and introduces a number of the more important symbols:

> The sky is a thin transparent blue, a very light blue merging into white, with stars in regular order, and a full moon. At the back center is a marble pavillion, small in distance against a regular black band of trees; on either side is a slender poplar tree in graceful silhouette. Both wings are closed by sections of wall covered with roses; motionless on the left wall is a peacock, black against the lighter sky. In the middle foreground is a pool and a fountain [pp. 1-2].[20]

---

[20] Millgate, *Achievement*, p. 8, quotes the text of this paragraph from the reproduction of it in Meriwether, *Literary Career*, as Figure 1. I am quoting from one of the two Texas copies, each of which has a text slightly different, in stylistic matters, mostly, from each other and from the copy reproduced in *Literary Career*. My quotations are from what I will arbitrarily call the First Texas Copy; the Second Texas Copy, for the record, has the following dedication: TO "CHO-

The second paragraph of the opening description is a verbal portrait of the accompanying drawing, which is reproduced as Figure 1 of Meriwether's *Literary Career,* and introduces us to the completely dissipated major character, Pierrot, whose physical and apparently emotional disorder is juxtaposed to the formally ordered and maintained setting—the "regular order" of the stars and "regular" trees:

> Pierrot is seated at right front, in a fragile black chair beside a delicate table. His left arm is curved across the table top, his right arm hangs at his side, and his head rests upon his curved arm, face toward front. He appears to be in a drunken sleep. There is a bottle and an overturned wineglass upon the table, a mandolin and a woman's slipper lie at his feet. He is dressed in white and black, flung across the chair is a scarf of black and gold Chinese brocade. He does not move during the play [pp. 2-3].

The concluding statement that Pierrot "does not move during the play" is structurally very important; it draws our attention immediately and somewhat enigmatically back to the list of "persons" in the play, which lists not just "Pierrot," but "Shade of Pierrot" as well. Thus the drunken clown Pierrot, onstage throughout, would seem to be the operative figure in the play, and the implication is certainly very strong that the subsequent action takes place in Pierrot's head, either as a dream of himself as the would-be lover, like Mallarmé's (and Faulkner's) faun waking from his dreams of conquest, or as a guilt-ridden dream of remorse over damage he has done to the formerly innocent Marietta.

The stage thus set, the two principal commentators, who appear at each important juncture in the play, enter; called the Grey Figure and the Lilac Figure in the list of persons, they are identified when they speak only as "First Figure" and "Second Figure." They enter in a "slightly unnatural rythm" (p. 3), which suggests their thematic kinship to Pierrot—they are, as we learn, his servants—and their alienation from the formal atmosphere of the garden; they come front and begin, paradoxically, to make highly formal and ornate

---

CHO,"/A TINY FLOWER OF THE FLAME, THE/ETERNAL GESTURE CHRYSTALLIZED;/THIS, A SHADOWY FUMBLING IN/WINDY DARKNESS, IS MOST RE-/SPECTFULLY TENDERED/FIRST EDI-TION 1920.

speeches which are filled with elaborate similes—much like the dialogue between the Page of Herodias and the Young Syrian in the opening pages of Oscar Wilde's *Salomé*. The First Figure calls attention to the stillness in the garden: "How still it is! The air does not stir, the air is like a candle flaming in a dusky colonnade" (pp. 3-4); but the Second Figure argues that it is not still: "The sky is like a blue candle flame, the sky is a curtain of thin blue silk and the wind stirs it like a white hand" (p. 4).

It soon becomes clear, however, that the disagreement has nothing really to do with whether there is, in fact, wind blowing or not, but with their differing ways of perceiving and responding to the world—in this case, the garden, but later, also, to Marietta and her situation. The First Figure appears to see only the externalities, the rigid formality and artificiality of the garden, and his speeches are filled with images of death and violence; but the Second Figure seems, at this point, to be aware that it is, after all, a garden, and that underneath the cold and clipped rigidity, underneath the statues, things do live and die; his speeches, consequently, are filled with images of life. When the First Figure, for example, argues that "The sky itself is still" and that "the stars are like silver apples pasted on thin blue silk" (p. 4), the Second responds with a rather nice series of images which personify the sky:

> The stars are like gardenias before they turn brown from the heat of a human body; the sky is like thin blue silk stirring upon a living breast. Why does the sky stir like silk with breathing? It is like the covered breast of a woman kneeling between two candles, and the moon is a flat Roman coin suspended upon her breast [pp. 4-5].

To this the First Figure counters two intentionally harsh and shocking similes, one paraphrasing "Prufrock," which reinforce his vision of the garden world as sterile and unlovely: "The moon is like a dismembered breast upon the floor of a silent sea," he says; "the moon is like the bloated face of a scorned woman who has drowned herself. How still it is!" (pp. 5-6). The twin poplars described in the opening become, for the Second Figure, "like two blind virgins" that "sway in unison like two violin bows," and even the nine columns of the colonnade become "nine muses standing like votive candles around a blue mountain" (p. 6); while to the First Figure those poplars are like *"statues* of virgins in dark green bronze" whose shadows are unreal and dimensionless like "the reflections of two candles in a flat mirror" (p. 7; my emphasis).

The real point of dissension, the real question at stake, is the paradox which the symbol of the formal garden contains: that is, to what extent can Nature, so carefully ordered and controlled, remain Nature, and perpetuate life? The question is, of course, one of the major themes of Faulkner's great fiction —*Go Down, Moses,* for example, and *Requiem for a Nun*— where he uses the Wilderness and the Community as metaphors for Freedom and Bondage. On a human level, the question is the extent to which the individual can submit to society's rules and still remain free. Absolute freedom for the individual in a society can only result in anarchy and chaos—witness the results of Nancy Mannigoe's disregard of the law, of Charlotte Rittenmeyer's disregard of convention, and of Temple Drake's disregard of both—and so it is essential that society enforce certain rules of behavior: but at what point do the rules, the controls, the formalities, actually destroy the life they were meant to nurture and sustain? The whole theme is a tremendously important one in Faulkner's work, and it is significant to see him working with it at the beginning of his career, even though on the much smaller scale.

The formal garden, then, is the over-riding symbol of *Marionettes;* its ordered, regular seasonal change is an effective bass-line to the urges, the desires and passions, which move the characters in the drama. And the extended, contrasting descriptions of it in the first few pages function not just to introduce Marietta, the soon-to-be-betrayed, but to draw attention to the kinship that exists between Marietta and the garden itself. In *Prunella,* the play which has been mentioned as a probable source for *Marionettes,* there is a particular exchange of dialogue which quite specifically defines the symbolic function of the garden there; by extension, or even just analysis, it applies to *Marionettes* as well. Prunella, very much like Marietta, hidden from the outside world behind a high wall, enters the stage preparing for her "lesson," her daily recitation

of the aphorisms of modest living which the aunts require of
her. She encounters the gardener, at work; asks him what he
is doing; and his answer, made while he continues clipping the
hedge, implies that he is doing for the garden what the aunts
are trying to do for Prunella:

> PRUNELLA. What are you doing there?
> 3rd GAR. Giving Nature a lesson, miss.
> PRUNELLA. What are you teaching her?
> 3rd GAR. To keep straight! I'll let her know who's master while
> *I'm* here.
> PRUNELLA. And if you didn't, what would happen?
> 3rd GAR. Why, she'd kick over the traces and be off her own way
> in no time. She's bad enough as it is, always getting herself
> [*clips*] out of shape, and trying to be different to what you make
> her. [*Clips.*] Well, that you can't help, you've just got to come
> along and put it right. [*Clips.*] First she'll run to leaf—that
> you can't help—then she'll run to seed—that you can't help—
> then she goes stalky [*clips*] rots herself— dies and stinks.
> None of it you can't help.
> PRUNELLA. What can you do, then?
> 3rd GAR. Oh, you—you—can make things uncomfortable for her;
> you can show her what she ought to be, and keep her in her
> place—make her toe the line. That's what a garden's for, that's
> where gardening comes in.[21]

Thus the purpose of the garden, its symbolic function, is to
bridle Nature, to control it; the purpose of "instruction" is to
bridle passion. It is the over-instruction, the over-protection,
of certain individuals—Miss Zilphia Gant, Howard Boyd, and
Temple Drake are examples—which creates the imbalance between freedom and restraint, and which therefore throws both
Nature and Civilization into chaos. Likewise, it is the over-
protection of both Prunella and Marietta that renders them
unable to cope with the devices of a scoundrel like Pierrot.

One thinks immediately of at least two other formal gardens
in Faulkner's fiction: of the garden of the marble faun, who
is totally incapable, though he would, of giving way to his passions, and the formal garden in *Soldiers' Pay,* which forms
such an important part of the symbolic structure of that book.
Margaret Yonce is right, I think, in her suggestion that "its
very formality serves a symbolic function by placing it out-

---

21 *Prunella,* pp. 11-12.

side the ordinary realm of activity,"[22] but it also symbolizes
the restrictive controls which Reverend Mahon, who created
the garden, and Margaret Powers, who loves to walk in it, have
placed over their own emotional lives—Reverend Mahon who,
according to Yonce, "has withdrawn into his garden where life
flows about him without affecting him,"[23] and Mrs. Powers,
who is not able to give herself completely, for many different
reasons, to anyone. By way of contrast it is also worth noting
that about the time of *Soldiers' Pay,* in his unfinished and unpublished novel *Elmer,* Faulkner describes Paris, that Western
symbol for all that is voluptuous and sensual and unrestrained,
as a "homely *informal* garden."[24]

Like the garden, then, Marietta displays a cold and formal
exterior which has been developed and nurtured, apparently,
by her "three grey aunts" as an external control over her
emotions, in their well-intended efforts to help her keep from
making the same mistake her mother had made; Marietta, as
a result, is actually seething inside with an urge, specifically
sexual, which she can neither fully understand nor cope with.
She enters stage dressed in white, but before speaking she
makes three symbolically significant gestures: she pauses at the
fountain, associating herself very early with the already accumulating number of narcissus images, which are to be so
important in understanding the latter part of the play; she
then "faces the moon and raises her arms with a quick gesture"
(p. 8), making obeisance to all of the moon's paradoxical and
symbolic meanings: as symbol of love and beauty; as symbol
of the chaste and sterile, but beautiful, huntress; and as symbol
of the cold aloofness of the powers that created the world, the
insignificance of man—*la lune ne garde aucune rancune.* Finally,
she "goes to the rose bush at left, and draws an armful of
them about her face" (p. 8), a gesture which might be inter-
preted, especially in light of her speech, which follows immediately, as an unconscious identification with Nature, an
expression of the health and rightness of the sexual urges which
she feels; but conjoined with the narcissus images, with the

---

[22] Yonce, p. 48. Her complete discussion of the garden covers pp.
47-49.

[23] Yonce, p. 52.

[24] Quoted in Millgate, *Achievement,* p. 21. My italics.

peacocks which adorn the stage, and, finally, with specific images of her vanity in the last part of the play, the gesture rather implies that she is using the roses primarily as self-decoration.

The gestures, then, suggest the ambivalence in her character; and the ambivalence is nicely symbolized by the disparity between the mechanical formality of her diction and her movements on stage—when speaking she stands, like a marionette, "in a slightly strained but graceful attitude" (p. 9)—and the emotional intensity which her actual words express:

> I cannot sleep, my narrow bed is not cool tonight. My bed is no longer comfortable, it has filled me with strange desires, for vague, unnamed things. Why cannot I sleep tonight? Is it because a singing voice disturbed my dream? But I do not know, I cannot know the voice which sang beneath my window. No, no, I do not want to know! am afraid to know! Am I afraid, I wonder? But my nightingales, they are afraid of the singing voice. The nightingales that once sang in my garden have flown, my garden is like a room when the candles are extinguished. Am I afraid of a darkened room? Oh, but it is something else: my bed has drawn sleep from my body as a stone wall draws dew from the roses that cover it. My bed is like the breast of a peasant woman heated with labor in August vineyards, and the air in my room is shadowy with echoes like dying ripples, faint as the scent of honey suckle at dusk. I cannot sleep in my room tonight. How still it is! There is no sound save the liquid gold nightingales; the liquid calls of the nightingales ebb and flow across my face with faint, sound like tiny waves upon a moonlit beach. How still it is! and cool, but I am not cool, and my hands are hot as magnolia petals at noon and my body is hot like the earth in a sun drenched garden. How cool the pool looks! It is like a naked girl lying among the roses; it is so cool that I shall cool my face and my hands in it. There is no one here, dare I bathe in this pool? [pp. 9-12].

Several things are worth noting in her speech: first is her anxiety, her "strange desires, for vague, unnamed things," which she traces directly to her "narrow bed," a phrase Faulkner borrowed from his own adaptation of Verlaine's "Fantoches," in which the half-naked daughter of the Doctor of "Bogona" "Glides trembling from her narrow bed" for a sexual tryst with her "lover waiting in the moon."[25] The "singing voice" which disturbs her is obviously the voice of her emotions, long re-

---

[25] *Early Prose and Poetry*. p. 57.

pressed; the nightingales, which are, from the context, apparently related to those "melodious but slightly tiresome nightingales in a formal clipped hedge" which Faulkner referred to a couple of years later,[26] have fled, as Marietta flees, from that emotion: that is, Marietta's anxiety, which she does not allow to become actual frustration, is caused by her fear that she might be losing control of herself, entering the world of experience, and thereby sacrificing the order which her life has known. Further, to her, as to Quentin Compson nearly a decade later, the honeysuckle is an impetus to her urging sexuality, and she feels her body, restless from sleeplessness, and, very much like Dewey Dell Bundren's, "hot like the earth in a sun drenched garden," to be in direct conflict with the emotionless garden. Significantly, she suppresses her anxieties in the pool, cooling her ardor in another narcissistic gesture— "She approaches the pool undecided, then with a single movement she slips out of her gown and steps slowly into the water" (p. 12)—which, again, symbolically anticipates her sterile, self-contemplating vanity, and the death of her soul, in the final scene.

While she is "cooling" herself, the voice which she has been hearing becomes audible; it is the voice of Pierrot, or the "Shade of Pierrot," apparently, and a chorus, singing "beyond the wall." Pierrot's song of seduction is not notable for any real poetic quality, but it is perfectly appropriate to both the play and the character of Pierrot. The lyric, while lifeless, is very rhythmic and spirited, though in a jerky and irregular sort of way: it is well-suited to the character of the marionette whom one imagines dancing, in counterfeited liveliness, to pulled strings, just across the wall:

Voice—   I am Pierrot, and was born
            On a February morn
            In Paris town, and on my head
            The moon shone, weaving in my head
            A spell, and till I am dead—
Chorus—   And from then till we are dead
            We have moon madness in the head,
            We have moon madness in the head.

---

[26] "American Drama: Inhibitions," *Early Prose and Poetry,* p. 95.

Voice—   Every month when comes the moon,
            I leave my musty garret room
            When she has cast her clothes away
            To naked dream 'till break o' day.
Chorus—   While she dreams the night away,
            We play at love 'till break o' day,
            We play at love 'till break o' day.
Voice—   She calmly watches me below,
            I am not calm, but to and fro
            I sing and whirl and leap and dance.
            Away all debts and toil I prance—
Chorus—   We sing and whirl and leap
                        and dance
            To mandolin's high dissonance
            To mandolin's high dissonance.
Voice—   The roses nod to me and sigh.
            The moon sits naked in the sky.
            The cold is gone, tis month o' May
            I seek some one to come and play.
Chorus—   We seek some one to come and
                        play.
            Tomorrow is another day,
            Tomorrow is another day.
Voice—   My foster mother dreams above.
            This night was made to sing and love.
            Your high shut garden tempted us,
            Heres music for our revelry—
Chorus—   Your high shut garden tempted us,
            O fair sweet maid, come dance
                        with us.
            O fair sweet maid come dance
                        with us! [pp. 13-16].

Specifically, then, Pierrot is the incarnation of Marietta's unconscious desires. He identifies himself with the moon, to which
Marietta has just offered supplication, and by injecting himself,
the "high dissonance" of his mandolin, into the garden, he
threatens to disturb its stately formality; by injecting passion
into Marietta's waking consciousness, he threatens to disturb
the cool regularity of her life: he does both. Leaping upon the
wall he begins to sing directly to her: "You are a trembling
pool," he tells her, in part, "And I am a flame that only you
can quench. . . . /Let me drown myself between your breast
points,/ Beloved" (pp. 18-19).

To the song, the significance of which will be discussed later,

in another context, Marietta listens, "frightened," making the
formal gesture of clasping her hands across her breast, even
though, so far as the text tells us, she is still in the water, still
naked, and "hypnotized" by Pierrot. Confronted so directly by
her desires, she retreats, perhaps instinctively, to the security
which order and regularity have given her up till now, and
her reply, unlike the fairly impassioned, anxious prose of her
opening speech, is in very clipped and formal, controlled iambic
tetrameter couplets:

> No, no, kind sir, I cannot
> > dance!
> I know not how, for my three aunts
> Told me my mother went this way,
> Slipped from her room at break of day
> Because a stranger sang to her
> Beneath her window on a night
> Like this, blue velvet and moonlight.
> [She was scarce as old as I]
> Then she returned, my mother sweet,
> And slow and sad were her white feet,
> Yet slower still, and from her
> > grave
> There sprang a flower, sweet and
> > brave.
> The flower was I, so say my aunts,
> And I must never learn to dance.
> O please dont make me want to try! [pp. 20-21].

The refusal, however, is so formal and deliberate as to seem
almost rote: there is a sense, certainly justified by the character she becomes, in which she is indeed protesting too much,
merely going through the motions of refusal, while actually
planning, perhaps not even consciously, to accept all along. At
any rate, after a single refusal, she is easily convinced, and sub-
mits to Pierrot's invitation. He invites her to "come without
regretting," and, as she reaches the wall, he reaches down, lifts
her up, and, like the puppets Scaramouche and Pulcinella in
Verlaine's "Fantoches"—but not in Faulkner's adaptation of it—
they make "a single black shadow on the moon" (p. 25), as if
to emphasize the coldness and sterility of the relationship they
are entering upon, again implying *la lune ne garde aucune
rancune*. They leave the stage together, to the fading sound of
Pierrot's final song, which is clearly a song of conquest:

My foster mother in the sky,
See my bright limbs flashing by!
I shake my hair, I stamp my feet,
And this maiden, grave and sweet,
This slender maiden, shivery white,
A rosebud shaken by moonlight!
Twist your fingers in her hair
Spin and weave moon madness there.
Spin your dreams within her head
And let them dance in her white bed
Till all her dreams are fever hot.
Rout peace until she knows it not,
But only madness in the head,
Desire to follow where I lead,
And dance and dance if so I wish,
While nightingales in every bush
Strew silver sequins, to enhance
My mandolin's high dissonance [pp. 25-26].

Immediately following the song, with its images of revelrous, impassioned living, the scene changes, auguring ill, thematically, for Marietta: the "moon disappears behind a cloud, leaving the stage in darkness;" the grey and lilac figures are seen "dimly" on stage, and, to the accompaniment of the "low tones of a violin," discuss the sudden change of season: "It is sudden cold, do you feel how cold it has become?" the First Figure says; he calls attention to the dying trees, and then announces that the "spirit of Autumn" is in the garden. The Second Figure's response is a laconic agreement, but it is loaded with significance which will become clear later: "Yes," he says, "the leaves are dying. All things must die, and dead things are heavy" (pp. 27-28).

The interlude which follows is perhaps the most distinctive structural feature of *Marionettes,* and specifically anticipates one of Faulkner's favorite fictional devices, the bold insertion into a work of an episode either slightly digressive from the main narrative, like the horsethief episode in *A Fable,* or completely divorced from it, like the "Old Man" sections of *The Wild Palms,* which serves as a thematic counterpoint to the main plot. The episode here parallels the story of Pierrot and Marietta, and anticipates, by implication, the unhappy ending to their affair; it is an allegorical story in which the "garden nymph," apparently thriving in the fullness of her garden's growing, her breasts "like two birds in the shadow of her hair, and her long, fair hair [hanging] down and the moon . . . combed throug[h] it like spun silver" (p. 30) as her lover, a personified "Summer," leaves her garden—abandons her, that is, as Pierrot is bound to abandon Marietta, "striding along the soft dim sky, his flushed face . . . lifted and his head . . . bound with lilac stalks" (pp. 29-30).

It is a kind of fabliau of the seasons,[27] and, narrated by the spirit of Autumn, the image and spirit of mortality, is rife with the sense of the necessity of change and the inevitability of death. The spirit of Autumn does not, for example, attribute their parting to any kind of dissatisfaction with each other— "They have not quarrelled," he says. "I am sure they have not quarrelled, yet she is sad; she is filled with a foreboding of disaster . . ." (p. 30)—but only to the inexorable workings of Time, to which the seasons are as subject as human beings. Summer even challenges, "for a fleeting second," the mechanism of change, and when he hears the nymph's voice calling after him, he stops, "half turned toward her, and for a fleeting second, he is the utter master of his soul: fate and the gods stand aloof watching him, his destiny waits wordless at his side." But even though the possibility of Free Will is offered him, "He goes on," like the puppet he is, "his eyes ever before him, looking into the implacable future" (p. 32).

It is also more than a fabliau of the seasons, for the spirit of Autumn's commentary invests it with a thematic significance directly related to the story of Pierrot and Marietta, and with even broader significance for Faulkner's later works. The spirit of Autumn suggests that there are reasons for Summer's refusal to return to the garden besides mere callousness:

> Perhaps a newer, stronger love has called him away, that he does not return: perhaps he is fallen upon by beasts while traversing a dark forest, or perhaps while crossing a stream he slipped and was drowned [pp. 32-33].

The syntactical structure, the colon following "return," in this

---

[27] Both Millgate, *Achievement,* p. 8, and Collins, *Early Prose and Poetry,* p. 18, suggest that the episode, narrated by the spirit of Autumn, is about Pierrot and Marietta; but it is so only by implication.

passage indicates that the parallel "perhaps" clauses actually identify the "newer, stronger love" which has called Summer away. The implications are significant: the first, that the "newer, *stronger* love" is actually death itself, anticipates and sets up Marietta's statement, when she returns, that "nothing save death" is as beautiful as she is; the second, related to it, is in Summer's narcissistic death by drowning: one immediately thinks of Bayard Sartoris, for example, Narcissa Benbow, and, as Carvel Collins has pointed out,[28] Quentin Compson, all of whom destroy themselves in one way or another, Quentin specifically by drowning, with their constant, nearly exclusive reflections on themselves. The most important implication, however, the larger one, is the fatalistic pall cast over the entire world by the fact that here, at any rate, it is Summer, the very Life Force itself, which is in love with death, and which has, at least according to the spirit of Autumn's interpretation, destroyed itself in contemplation of itself.

The remainder of the spirit of Autumn's narrative more or less confirms this view of the interlude. The garden nymph now "waits in vain" for Summer's return, in the dead garden, "among her dried rose stalks" (p. 33). "Her warning of disaster was a true warning," says the spirit of Autumn, "the disaster had come to pass" (p. 34). He then repeats the refrain of the song she had earlier sung when Summer left her, when she had sent "her heart after him," in a nicely turned phrase, "across the sweet pagan heart break of the September night" (pp. 30-31), but which now is much more poignant and thematically relevant: "Though love ever call and call,/He will not hear at all" (p. 34). The spirit of Autumn then explains: "no matter what faces bend above him, or what mouths sing to his unheeding ears," he will not hear. In his concern for himself, then, his constant seeking for new sensations, self-satisfaction, his love of death, Summer has cut himself off from any real relationship, from Love. The episode ends with an image of the moon as Narcissus, which more than anything else defines the meaning of the symbol of the moon in the entire play. The garden nymph sits alone with her sorrow, while

[28] *Early Prose and Poetry,* p. 18.

the half moon in the sky star[e]s blank face to blank face, with the half moon in the stream [p. 34].

Indeed, yet again, *la lune ne garde aucune rancune.*

The garden to which Marietta returns, then, is a dead garden, dominated by the spirit of Autumn, the spirit and symbol of Dying if not of Death, who remains silently on the wall during the play's final scene, supplying a "background in a single tone against which the succeeding action takes place. Without moving or speaking, he dominates the whole scene" (p. 35). That is, all of the remaining actions are imbued with the sense of death, of dying, and of sterility.

Marietta is preceded on stage by the Grey and Lilac Figures who, once again in agreement with each other, emphasize the autumnal nature of the setting, in a rather eloquent series of exchanges:

> First Figure— It is autumn. The autumn will strip this garden, but the garden itself will not change, for it is old, it has felt the chill of a thousand winters. But all things must grow old, we do not grow old alone. The earth is already old, the earth is like an aged woman gathering fagots in a barren field. Soon snow will streak her face with quiet tears; but there are no tears in the earth's eyes now; she is blind with things that she has seen. There are no more gapemouthed crocuses, or poppies wide with woe to wreath her fingers; the earth is a hunched and sightless woman, holding herself together with her hair.
> Second Figure— Hither comes the ghosts of stripped springs grown old and dumb and sightless, and here come also, winds from blue Ionic hills over which the sunlight spills its muted gold, yet the hills are bare of any life, the fearful sheep gather in fold against the winter, subtle as a beast, and keen and cold [pp. 35-37].

Age, sterility, and death: the birds are gone and, as the First Figure puts it, in one of *Marionettes'* most sharply focussed images, ". . . the passing days scatter like petals on the ground as quietly as shattered roses, like sweet and sad and endless repetitions of a name" (pp. 37-38). The Second Figure responds with two significant images. The first is directly related to "Study," a poem Faulkner wrote about the same time and published in *The Mississippian,* in which a student, whose every instinct is responding to the sensual, burgeoning Spring world outside his window, wishes that he "were a bust/All head" so that he can concentrate more completely on his studies.[29] In *Marionettes* the image is applied directly to the statues in the garden, which "are not cold" because they "are all head" (p. 38). They are fit inhabitants of such a garden, then, literally, because of their lifelessness; metaphorically, the image suggests the suppression of the body, the feelings, the passions, by an act of the mind, which, as we shall see, is what Marietta, upon returning, will have done to herself. The Second Figure's other comment is an image of death, which stands in direct complement to the spirit of Autumn's closing image of the moon as Narcissus: "The leaves shake from the blond boughs and slide down the sky hill, and the moon, even the moon is a dead leaf, blown across the sky" (p. 38).

Under this dead, narcissistic moon, with the spirit of Autumn dominating the background, Marietta reappears, completely changed—at least externally. Wearing a "flame colored gown," as opposed to the white gown she wore on her first appearance, she "comes to the front, looking about her as if she had never seen the garden before" (p. 39). She is apprehensive at the changes, both in the garden and in herself: "How this garden has changed!" she observes. "Why has it changed so? Ah I know, it is the autumn that has changed the garden. But I am not changed. Am I changed very much, I wonder?" (p. 39). As before, she immediately suppresses her emotional agitation by looking at her own reflection in the pool.

While she studies her own image, the Grey and Lilac Figures, who hid themselves when she reappeared, begin to discuss her, and in their reactions to her at this point they cease being merely chorus and become characters in their own right; and the relationship between them is worth a short word, since their disagreements form one of the structural elements of the play, and add a significant if minor thematic dimension to *Marionettes*. For in the beginning the reader tends to react less favorably to the First Figure, who is, after all, the one who describes the garden with images of death and dismemberment, and more favorably to the Second Figure, who rather, at least apparently, sees life there. During this final exchange, however, it becomes clear that these initial impressions of

---

[29] *Early Prose and Poetry*, pp. 62-63.

them are wrong; for here both agree that Marietta is beautiful (p. 44), even though they describe her in completely different terms. But the Second Figure, it becomes clear, admires her only as one admires an *objet d'art*: "She is like an ivory tower builded by black slaves and surrounded by flames, she is like a little statue of ivory and silver for which blood has been spilt" (p. 41); her "hair is gold, it is like the gold of a galleon captured by pirates, gold bleached with blood and passion" (p. 42); and "her eyes are like pools in which one could drown oneself, her breast is a narrow white pool also, and her breast points are like reflections of twin stars. Her breasts are ivory crusted jewels for which men have died, for which armies have slain one another and for which brother has murdered brother" (p. 43). That is, she is beautiful to him precisely because of her gaudy artificiality, and even because of the potential of death and violence which she emanates. Apparently, then, his earlier pleasure in the garden was not at all in his response to natural beauty, as it then seemed, but in his admiration of its clipped and combed, cool and regular formality; he responds to Art, then, as he does not respond to Life.

The First Figure, however, who saw only death in the garden, sees Marietta here as the fragile image of life itself, "like a slender birch tree stripped by a storm, she is a birch tree shivering at dawn upon the dim border of a wood, no she is a young poplar between a white river and a road" (pp. 41-42);[30] her hair "is like the sun on a field of wheat, it is like sunlight combed through maple leaves" (p. 42). He resented the garden earlier, then, apparently because he saw it as restrictive of Nature and therefore life-denying; by the same token he understands Marietta, under all of the decoration, to be a vulnerable, and hurt, human being. His response, then, throughout the play, is more directly to Life than to Art, and it is therefore he, rather than the Second Figure, who is the healthiest character in the play.

The point is not at all an unimportant one, for Faulkner seems here to be making a comment about the function of Art which has at least some significance for his own career as

---

[30] Faulkner also used this phrase in his poem "A Poplar," *Early Prose and Poetry*, p. 60.

an artist: it is not very difficult to see in the Second Figure
Faulkner's implicit criticism of the "Art for Art's Sake" movement, with its emphasis on, and sterile contemplation of, form,
color, and control, a kind of narcissism in itself, which denied
that life had any real meaning outside of Art. Michael Millgate has well said that "Faulkner's major concerns, like those
of all great artists, were ultimately moral, and there is little
value in abstract discussions of his ideas which fail to take
this into account,"[31] and it strikes me that Faulkner was even
here, this early in his career, at least indirectly voicing that
moral concern with the problems of being human, which is at
the root of all of his mature writing.

At any rate, their discussion of Marietta forms a fine choral
counterpoint to her own comments as she stares at herself in
the pool: " . . . I am not changed. I am really beautiful now"
(p. 41); and the content of her comments seems to indicate
that they are both right about her: she is a vulnerable, terribly
wounded character, and though she has externally changed, like
the garden itself, she is still the same person she has always
been. We are asked, then, to take her literally when she says
that she is not changed, and then to reinterpret her earlier
actions in the light of the way we see her now. Indeed, as I
have suggested, she has been associated with numerous images
of narcissism throughout the play; these images come to a point
here and in her long closing speech, in which she defines her
true character most directly. The implication is, of course, that
she is a vain and sterile character from the beginning; and,
possibly, that she succumbed to Pierrot not just because of his
romantic allure, but also simply because he was paying attention
to her, flattering her vanity—like Narcissa Benbow, for example,
in *Sartoris*, who refuses to destroy Byron Snopes's amatory letters, which simultaneously appall and stimulate her, because in
them she has concrete evidence that she is the object of some-
body's admiration.

Her final speech, which ends the play, is a long and intricately developed peroration, which sums up, restates, many
of the play's themes:

One grows old, beauty goes as the leaves slip earthward, without

---

[31] Millgate, *Achievement*, p. 287.

any sound. I too shall grow old, but I am beautiful now; nothing save death is as beautiful as I am. And I shall wear a gown of green jade, and I shall walk in the gravel paths of my formal garden. When I walk, the green motion of my gown will be repeated by the jade on my finger nails, and my hair will be heavy with gold, so that the weight of my hair will hurt my head. My temples will be smooth with gold also, and the gravel of the gravel paths will hurt my feet, and between the slight pain in my head and the slight pain in my feet will be jewels, and silver and dull gold cunningly chased by an Italian dying of tuberculosis, and the purple on my feet will be thick with jewels to rival the red points of my peacocks eyes, like the eyes of wolves upon a wood's edge. My peacocks are white and purple and they cry to their reflections in the bottomless pool below the cypress trees. And the lilacs beside the pool stare unstirringly at the lilacs within the pool until the cries of my peacocks shudder through them; then the lilacs beside the [pool]32 stir, and cry soundlessly to the lilacs within the pool. And the cypress trees struggle upward from the pool, and brush stars down into the garden.

I desire—What do I desire?

The wind smoothes the sky's hair smoothly back,

The wind combs the pines from grey to black, while the cacaphonous cries of my peacocks shudder through the ilex before the statue of Hermes.

The ilex is grey, it came from a white island in a sea of amethyst, and a wind streaked the sea with lapis-lazuli and faded the ilex grey. The ilex is grey like a grey wall and the statue of Hermes is a marble island in a sea of shadow, and the wind combs the sky grey and black.33

I shall sit on a grey wall, and I shall swing my painted legs through intricate figures; and my breasts, like twin moons that have been dead for a thousand years, will stare heavily over my girdle of dull brass into the garden where the moon streaks the shadow hair with silver; and my peacocks will follow me in voluptuous precision, brushing the moonlight from the path with their heavy tails. Their eyes will grow avid and thick and remorseless, like the eyes of virgins growing old; and they will approach and eat the jewels from my feet, and the jade clasps from my finger tips, and my heavy hair, and the gilded eyelids on my eyes will attract them while their cold feet mark my body with thin crosses.

I desire—What do I desire?

The wind streaks the moon's hair on the sky,

---

32 I am supplying the word "pool" from the Second Texas Copy.

33 These lines form something of a paraphrase of 11. 126-128 of "The Love Song of J. Alfred Prufrock." I am grateful to Stephen E. Meats for reminding me of this.

The moon will play my body when I die, and the cacaphonous
cries of my peacocks have blighted the ilex before the statue of
Hermes.

Curtain [pp. 46-51].

The passage is full of images of narcissism, of course. The
repeated emphasis on weight and heaviness—her hair so "heavy
with gold" that it will hurt her head—specifically recalls the
Second Figure's earlier comment that "dead things are heavy"
(p. 28), and the image of her breasts as "twin moons that have
been dead for a thousand years [staring] heavily over [her]
girdle" recalls also the First Figure's narcissistic image of the
moon as "like a dismembered breast upon the floor of a silent
sea . . . like the bloated face of a scorned woman who has
drowned herself" (pp. 5-6). The numerous images of Death,
Vanity, and Narcissism culminate in the fine Waste Land symbol
of the "grey," ashy, ilex surrounding the marble-bound Hermes,
and the play ends with the interesting and suggestive image of
the cold and sterile moon's "playing" Marietta's cold and sterile
body, and with the specific information that the formerly alive
and green ilex has been "blighted" by the "cacaphonous cries"
—like Pierrot's mandolin's "dissonance"—of the vain and voluptuous peacocks: all of which reinforce, in the final paragraph,
the play's theme that narcissism, selfishness, is, indeed, a form
of Death.

Marietta emerges, then, at the end of the play, recognizably
as type and symbol, perhaps even twentieth-century avatar,
of a kind of woman who appears frequently in the decadent
literature of the late nineteenth century—Gautier's Cleopatra
and Flaubert's Salammbô, for example[34]—who are corruptions
of the female principle. More specifically, Faulkner seems to
be here alluding to and even borrowing from, Wilde's *Salomé*
and Mallarmé's *Hérodiade,* both portraits of such women. The
borrowings from *Salomé* are not quite so direct as those from
Hérodiade, but are, I think, very real: I have already, for
example, suggested that the dialogue between the grey and
lilac figures is in the manner of the opening dialogues of *Salomé;*

---

[34] Cf. the chapter entitled "Byzantium" in Mario Praz, *The Romantic
Agony,* trans. Angus Davidson. Second Edition, London, 1970, for a
thorough discussion of the background of this type of woman, for
numerous examples, and for leads for further study.

particularly interesting also is the fact that Herod, trying to dissuade Salomé from her insistence upon having the head of Jokanaan, offers her, first, all of his "beautiful white peacocks," which bear a remarkable resemblance to those Marietta describes: "Their beaks are gilded with gold, and the grains that they eat are gilded with gold also, and their feet are stained with purple. When they cry out the rain comes, and the moon shows herself in the heavens when they spread their tails."[35] That failing, Herod offers her jewels:

> . . . jewels that are marvellous. I have a collar of pearls, set in four rows. They are like unto moons chained with rays of silver. They are like fifty moons caught in a golden net. On the ivory of her breast a queen has worn it. Thou shalt be as fair as a queen when thou wearest it. I have amethysts of two kinds, one that is black like wine, and one that is red like wine which has been coloured with water. I have topazes, yellow as are the eyes of tigers, and topazes that are pink as the eyes of a woodpigeon, and green topazes that are as the eyes of cats. I have opals that burn always with an ice-like flame, opals that make sad men's minds, and are fearful of the shadows. I have onyxes like the eyeballs of a dead woman. . . .[36]

More important, however, is the pervasive image of the moon, not just in the passages quoted, but throughout the play, to whom Salomé, like Marietta, makes obeisance when she first appears:

> How good to see the moon. She is like a little piece of money, you would think she was a little silver flower. The moon is cold and chaste. I am sure she is a virgin, she has a virgin's beauty. Yes, she is a virgin. She has never defiled herself. She has never abandoned herself to men, like the other goddesses.[37]

And the page of Herodias comments, when Salomé desires to have Jokanaan brought before her, in anticipation of the tragedy that is imminent, "Oh! How strange the moon looks. You would think it was the hand of a dead woman who is seeking to cover herself with a shroud."[38] That Marietta is, of course, fully capable of the cruelty and violence of Salomé is directly implied

---

[35] *The Works of Oscar Wilde* (London, 1963), p. 199.
[36] *The Works of Oscar Wilde*, p. 200.
[37] *The Works of Oscar Wilde*, p. 186.
[38] *The Works of Oscar Wilde*, p. 187.

both in the Second Figure's description of her, and in the image of voracity in Marietta's own description of her peacock's eyes as "like the eyes of wolves upon a wood's edge," and as growing "avid and thick and remorseless, like the eyes of virgins growing old."

The most specific borrowing, in so far as I can trace the sources, however, seems to be from *Hérodiade*. "Hérodiade," suggests Wallace Fowlie, in his fine book on Mallarmé, "is a soul seeking to escape from the state of becoming"—that is, like Marietta, from the state of flux, change—and that she "opposes the flow and the change of life by her studied and concentrated frigidity."[39] Like Marietta, Hérodiade is enamored of the "blonde torrent of [her] immaculate hair"[40] and tells her attendant nurse that her hairs "are not flowers/To spread forgetfulness of human ills,/But gold. . . ."[41] Also like Marietta she suggests that beauty is death,[42] and, looking into the mirror, which she addresses as "A cold water frozen with ennui,"[43] wonders "am I beautiful?"[44] Her attendant is very disturbed by her unwillingness to love, and asks her for whom she is keeping herself; her reply is almost a gloss on Marietta's final soliloquy:

H[érodiade].   For myself.
N[urse]. Sad flower which grows alone and has no other joy
          Than its own image seen in water listlessly.
          . . . .
H.   Besides, I want naught human, and if sculptured
          You see me with eyes lost in Paradise
          'Tis when I bring to mind your milk once drunk.
N.   Ah! Lamentable victim offered to its fate!
H.   Yes, it's for me, for me that I flower, deserted!
          You know it, gardens of amethyst, hid
          Endlessly in cunning abysses and dazzled,
          Ignored gold, keeping your antique light

---

[39] *Mallarmé* (Chicago, 1953), p. 127. This is a book which all Faulknerians should at least take a look at. Fowlie's chapter on "L'Après-Midi d'un Faune" is particularly interesting.

[40] *Stéphane Mallarmé: Poems*, trans. Roger Fry, (London, 1936), p. 79.

[41] Mallarmé, *Poems*, p. 81.

[42] Mallarmé, *Poems*, p. 79.

[43] Mallarmé, *Poems*, p. 81.

[44] Mallarmé, *Poems*, p. 83.

Under the sombre sleep of a primaeval soil,
You stones whence my eyes like pure jewels
Borrow their melodious brightness, and you
Metals which give my youthful tresses
A fatal splendour and their massive sway![45]

If Marietta, then, has direct literary connections with the sterile and life-denying Fatal Woman of late nineteenth-century literature, Pierrot, too, has specific literary ancestors other than the Harlequins, Pagliaccis, and other clowns of the *commedia dell'arte* tradition. If on the one hand we interpret the whole play as a guilt-ridden dream of remorse of the drunken Pierrot, who, asleep on the fragile stage table, "does not move during the play," Pierrot is, like Januarius Jones in *Soldiers' Pay,* a collateral, if not actually direct, descendant of James Branch Cabell's Jurgen, whose "indiscriminate lechery"[46] always leaves him unsatiated, unsatisfied, and unfulfilled. If, on the other hand, we understand the play as Pierrot's fantasy, a dream, of himself as the all-conquering, irresistible Lover, then he would seem to be more directly in the line of descent from the faun in Mallarmé's "L'Après-Midi d'un Faune," who dreams the same dream, and who, not incidentally, influenced at least three other Faulkner poems of approximately this period: his own "L'Apres-Midi d'un Faune," *The Marble Faun,* and an unpublished poem, a two-page fragment of which is preserved at the University of Texas. The fragment indicates that Faulkner had at one time planned to introduce into *The Marble Faun*—or at least into an early form of the poem which was to become Faulkner's first published book—a character much like the "Shade of Pierrot," a human "lover" to stand in direct complement to the growth and fecundity of the Nature around him, and in direct contrast to the statue's own lifelessness. He was, then, apparently, to represent to the faun the same thing that he represents to the sleeping Pierrot: the ideal embodiment of all his wishes to be sexually vigorous. The poem is narrated by a statue recognizably the marble faun, and eight lines actually appear in *The Marble Faun;*[47] the lyric appears in *Marionettes* in its entirety (pp. 17-19), as part of Pierrot's song of seduction:

---

[45] Mallarmé, *Poems,* p. 85.
[46] Millgate's phrase. *Achievement,* p. 64.
[47] *The Marble Faun and A Green Bough* (New York, 1968). *The*

Those cries, like scatt[ered silve]r sails,
Spread across an azure sea.
Her hands also caress me,
My keen heart also does she dare;
Plunging white fingers through my hair
While flocks of shining pleiades
Like ghostly Oceanides,
Turning always through the skies,
White feet mirrored in my eyes,
Weave a snare about my brain
Unbreakable by surge or strain.

The breathing dark stops suddenly,
Where one beneath a balcony
Masked, as his lute's trembling notes
Drift noiselessly like silver motes
In a moonbeam, breathes above,
A lover singing to his love:

Your little feet have crossed my heart,
              Love.
Your little white feet;
And I am a garden sprung beneath your footsteps.

You are a trembling pool,
              Love.
A breathless white pool;
And I am a flame that only you can quench.

Then we shall be one in the silence,
              Love.
The pool and the flame;
Till I am dead or you have become a flame.

Till you are a white delicate flame,
              Love.
A little slender flame
Drawing my hotter flame like will-o-the-wisp in my garden.

But now you are white and narrow as a pool,
              Love,
And trembling cool.
Let me drown myself between your breast points,
              Beloved.

So he sings. There is no bliss
In any mortal lover's kiss

Marble Faun, cf. p. 33; versions of ll. 1-4 and ll. 8-11 appear as part of the published work on this page. Also I have completed the fragmented first line by reference to the line as it is printed in this volume.

For me, a stone, half beast, half god.
The world turns sadly in my heart,
Dumb and blind, that only knows
[   ] burning of all winter snows. . . .

Ultimately, though, Faulkner seems to have intended, in Pierrot, to synthesize both types: the Jurgen-Don Juan-like Pierrot, for all of his sexuality, is actually no less sterile and life-denying than the impotent faun-like Pierrot, and both are guilty of the same kind of vain self-contemplation as Marietta. Indeed, Pierrot in his love song brings to specific point the whole thematic relationship between Vanity, Beauty, and Death, when he specifically identifies Marietta as a "pool" and invites himself to "drown," like Summer, between her "breast points." Pierrot and Marietta, then, are basically two sides of the same narcissistic coin, sterile and moribund in their selfish insistence on living exclusively for their own satisfacton.

*   *   *   *   *

Perhaps, finally, a word needs to be said about the title, which seems, unlike Faulkner's other titles, to be none too subtle in its rather pointed and perhaps sophomoric assertion that men are the playthings of Fate. And it would seem, from this angle, to be directly related to another unpublished and undated poem fragment, at the University of Texas, entitled "Two Puppets in a Fifth Avenue Win[dow]":

. . . Again he tautens, yellow, eternal [   ]
Again the other beneath him, staring at not[hing?]
Concentrates to the destiny that compels him [   ]
That impossibly articulates his arms.
Yellow he rises through pitiless jerking gradatio[ns?]
Yellow his face, swung downward and snared by elec-
    trics,
Unchanged, bloodlessly flouts Isaac Newton.
Terifically they poise to a parting of palms.

Then for a moment they hang there, gaudy and froze[n?]
A Spurious gesture of passion and flouted laws;
Till downward he swings in ludicrous surrender;
And to that force compelling them, they pause
And relaxed, forever above or below any laughter
Their faces, forever blind, stare through the elec-
    trics,
Implacably through distorted transparence of window

> Superbly still and sinister, before them at nothing [   ]
> And you, who on the pavement forever pass,
> Obeying without question forces that ever compel y[ou]
> You pause: for a moment you, too, are [   ]
> [   ]rgan of sight without brain, a g[   ]
>   to support it; . . . .

The abrupt shift of attention here to the human beings suggests, certainly, that there are distinct similarities between the humans and the puppets: the puppets controlled at every move by the strings, the human beings just as controlled, at every move, by "forces that . . . compel."

Unquestionably, Faulkner was interested in the notion of Fate, and in the image of men as puppets, particularly when he could use this notion and image to add both classical and tragic dimensions to his work; and perhaps the most moving and intricately articulated image of this type is Judith Sutpen's impassioned description of the hopelessness of the human condition:

> You get born and you try this and you dont know why only you keep on trying it and you are born at the same time with a lot of other people, all mixed up with them, like trying to, having to, move your arms and legs with strings only the same strings are hitched to all the other arms and legs and the others all trying and they dont know why either except that the strings are all in one another's way like five or six people all trying to make a rug on the same loom only each one wants to weave his own pattern into the rug; and it cant matter, you know that, or the Ones that set up the loom would have arranged things a little better, and yet it must matter because you keep on trying or having to keep on trying and then all of a sudden it's all over and all you have left is a block of stone with scratches on it. . . .[48]

And yet to assume too readily that *Marionettes* is purely Fatalistic, even with the spirit of Autumn's insistence, is to overlook completely the very real and fundamental human dimension in the play which I have tried to suggest: the viewpoint which posits, in the First Figure's sensitive and compassionate response to the returned Marietta, a moral scale against which each of the characters, marionette or not, can be measured. It would also be to overlook the fact that about two years later what Faulkner disliked most about Joseph Hergesheimer's novels was

---

[48] William Faulkner, *Absalom, Absalom!* (New York, 1951), p. 127.

precisely that his characters are merely "puppets he has carved and clothed and painted" and are part of "a terrific world without motion or meaning."[49] He particularly criticizes *Linda Condon* because it

> is not a novel. It is more like a lovely Byzantine frieze: a few unforgettable figures in silent arrested motion, forever beyond the reach of time and troubling the heart like music. His people are never actuated from within; they do not create life about them; they are like puppets assuming graceful but meaningless postures in answer to the author's compulsions, and holding these attitudes until he arranges their limbs again in other gestures as graceful and as meaningless.[50]

The over-riding impression in reading *Marionettes* is that its characters, at least in their creator's apprentice manner, *are* actuated from within, and therefore are not puppets at all. The singing voice that Marietta hears, her reaction to it, and Pierrot's rather studied and deliberate dissipation appear to me to be caused by what Faulkner described, over a decade later, as the old "gutful compulsions,"[51] a fine phrase loaded with significance for any discussion of Fate and Free Will in Faulkner's works.

The title, then, is metaphor: Fate is, to Faulkner, Consequence, the entangling accretion of actions and reactions to circumstance. And yet to say this is not at all to simplify. To think of man as the victim of forces he cannot control is to see him as a pitiable creature, a "puppet," indeed; to see him, however, as victim of forces, compulsions, that he *can* control, if he only would, seems, to me at any rate, not only to emphasize the moral dimension, but to complicate and darken the situation considerably. To whatever extent his characters, involved in a net of tragic circumstance, like Judith Sutpen, talk of Fate, to whatever extent they get comfort from placing responsibility on the shoulders of a "Puppet Master," it is nevertheless necessary for the reader to keep both the character and

---

[49] "Joseph Hergesheimer: Linda Condon—Cytherea—The Bright Shawl," in *Early Prose and Poetry*, p. 103.

[50] *Ibid.*, pp. 101-102.

[51] "Black Music," in *Doctor Martino and Other Stories* (New York, 1934), p. 263. It is worth noting, too, that Wilfred Midgleston, the story's central character, becomes, for one evening, a faun—or, as he puts it, a "farn."

the circumstance in the ever-present moral context in which Faulkner carefully places it. The gutful compulsions are human in origin, and whether they be Pride, Ambition, or simple Lechery, seem to me a form of narcissism, which, from a moral viewpoint, is simple selfishness: the concern with self to the exclusion of all meaningful human relationship, the distortion of human relationship in order to satisfy one's own needs and desires. And whether that selfishness takes the form, at the one extreme, of Pierrot's sad and self-defeating dissipation, or, at the other, of Marietta's sterile peacock-like adoration of her own heavily decorated and artificial image, or any of the gradations in between, the results, morally, are the same: the final drawing in *Marionettes,* the only one, so far as I can tell, which actually adds content to the text, is of Pierrot standing, staring at himself in a full-length mirror, rather like the spirit of Autumn's narcissistic moon staring "blank face to blank face" at itself in the pond, the apparently dead body of Marietta lying, supine, on a couch at his feet.

THOMAS L. McHANEY

Georgia State University

The Elmer Papers: Faulkner's Comic Portraits of the Artist

AFTER HE HAD submitted *Soldiers' Pay* to Boni and Liveright in 1925, William Faulkner left New Orleans, where he had been living since the first part of the year,[1] to make the young artist's obligatory pilgrimage to Europe. He was a confirmed writer of fiction by then. According to his traveling companion and New Orleans friend, the artist William Spratling, he wrote energetically on the freighter bound for Italy, although he destroyed some of what he set down during the long sea voyage.[2] After a misadventure in Italy—one which, like the trip itself, would find a way into Faulkner's fiction—the two young men separated. Spratling, who taught architectural drafting at Tulane and painted, went off on a tour of architectural sights, while Faulkner, who had a strong interest in the graphic arts himself, headed for Paris. He took a room on the Left Bank near the gallery that housed the paintings of the Impressionists and post-Impressionists, and wrote, among other things, a comical portrait of the artist as a young American. He called this work "Elmer," and he intended the story of his hero, a painter, to be a novel, but he never did complete it, saying much later that he gave up because the story was not funny enough.[3] The weakness of the humor was not the only problem with "Elmer," however, as the surviving typescript shows. Faulkner's characters proliferated and he often

---

[1] Michael Millgate, *The Achievement of William Faulkner* (New York: Random House, 1966), p. 20.

[2] The 1931 *Bookman* interview with Marshall J. Smith reports that Faulkner threw dozens of sonnets overboard (*Lion in the Garden: Interviews with William Faulkner, 1926-1962*, ed. James B. Meriwether and Michael Millgate [New York: Random House, 1968], p. 12). Spratling records in his autobiography that Faulkner brought a 4-inch MS on deck, tore it up and cast it overboard. (*File on Spratling* [Boston: Little, Brown, 1967], p. 31).

[3] James B. Meriwether, *The Literary Career of William Faulkner* (Princeton: Princeton University Library, 1961), p. 81.

foundered between comic and serious treatment, as if unsure
of his purpose.

"Elmer" failed, but it was not destroyed like the things
on the *West Ivis*. Faulkner saved the unfinished typescript,
and in the next decade he tried several times to salvage portions of the original conception. One early attempt was an
uncompleted short story entitled "Growing Pains," set, unlike
any of "Elmer," in Jefferson.[4] "Divorce in Naples"—recorded
on Faulkner's short story sending schedule in May 1930[5] and
first published in the 1931 collection *These 13*—also may date
from an earlier period. Somewhat later, to judge by fragmentary correspondence in the Faulkner collection at the University of Virginia, is a long unpublished story entitled "Portrait
of Elmer."[6] Besides these stories, which draw explicitly on
the unfinished novel, many characters, themes, and even patches
of dialogue and imagery from "Elmer" found a way into the
novels which followed, especially *Mosquitoes* (1927) and *Sartoris*
(1929). Then, much later, and with a high degree of seriousness, Faulkner took up the romantic—and apparently personal—

---

[4] One sheet among the Elmer papers now at Virginia bears, on both
sides, the title "Growing Pains." One version begins, "In Jefferson,
Miss., Elmer was in the fourth grade," and repeats an episode about
Elmer's infatuation with a boy who possessed "cruel beauty." This
version is less close than the version on the opposite side of the sheet
to the episode in the unfinished novel. William Oldenburg in his dissertation, "William Faulkner's Early Experiments with Narrative Technique," Michigan, 1966, suggests that this is the first appearance of
Jefferson in Faulkner's fiction, but it may not be, since other story
versions of the Elmer material appear to date from the 1930's, long
after Faulkner had "discovered" Jefferson in "Flags in the Dust,"
and "Growing Pains" may also date from that later time. Among the
papers recently discovered in Faulkner's Oxford home, Rowanoak,
were two MS pages representing different beginnings of "Growing
Pains," but I have not been able to examine them. (Information
supplied by Professor James B. Meriwether, who has examined copies
of the Rowanoak papers, in an interview May 13, 1973.)

[5] Meriwether, *Literary Career*, p. 171. The story was entitled
"Equinox" at the time of its first submission.

[6] Among the Elmer papers at Virginia are a number of incomplete
pages that represent trial drafts, apparently. One sheet entitled
"Elmer and Myrtle" may be a trial beginning of the novel or of a
short story; another, entitled "Portrait of Elmer Hodge," seems to
be a version of the short story rather than a new beginning of the
novel, as many have believed. Among the Rowanoak papers, according to Professor Meriwether, are miscellaneous pages of the "Elmer"
TS, including two versions of the ten pages missing from Book I at
Virginia. There is also an incomplete TS of "Portrait of Elmer."

elements of "Elmer" and gave them form in his 1939 novel *The Wild Palms,* where the love story of Harry and Charlotte echoes the affair between Elmer and Ethel in the 1925 attempt.

His continued use of the material indicates that "Elmer" remained important for Faulkner, even though he could not bring it off in the form he had originally projected. His problems with "Elmer" are typical of problems he solves with increasing skill in his early published work. There is an overriding problem of plot, of course; and "Elmer" may have been doomed from the moment the English aristocrats appear in Book III. The more typical problem is structural. As in other early novels, Faulkner strove in "Elmer" to develop proper strategies for unrolling his plot, for reconciling material and method. Consideration of his approach to the structure of "Elmer" reveals much about his developing sense of organic narrative form and throws new light on the major fiction which follows. In addition, "Portrait of Elmer," the unpublished story worked up from the unfinished novel after Faulkner had mastered his rapidly improving skills, is sufficiently interesting to warrant not only publication as a finished piece of fiction but serious discussion.

In both "Elmer" and "Portrait of Elmer," the would-be artist Elmer Hodge is the main character (as he is also the main character in the fragmentary "Growing Pains"). The novel and the long story open with an Elmer who is in his twenties and either bound for Paris ("Elmer") or arrived there ("Portrait"). Through flashbacks keyed to his present associations, his history is detailed. The following summary comes from "Elmer," but except for a few details that seem to have been intended for eventual revelation in the novel, it serves as his biography in "Portrait" as well.

Elmer Hodge is the youngest of four children in an itinerant Southern family. His father, like the Snopes schoolmaster in *The Hamlet* (1940), is an "inverted Io," a male wanderer "with hookworm and a passionate ambitious wife for gad-fly."[7] The

---

[7] "Elmer" TS, p. 18. The incomplete typescript has several gaps and pagination is not always sequential; several pages are not numbered at all. References to the TS will henceforth be within the body of the essay. They will follow the sequence of the papers at Virginia, numbered by Faulkner or coded by me as follows: 1-33; 44-51;

boy has several strong fixations. The color red, which will be important in his transformation to artist and painter, he associates first with the "red horror" of a burning house and the scarlet throats of his displaced, weeping brothers at the fire, as well as with the trauma of his appearing naked in the street at the time (TS, pp. 4-5). He is deeply attached to his older sister Jo-Addie, "with whom he slept, with whom he didn't mind being naked" (TS, p. 5). He admires phallic objects: the "simple slender shape in steel" of a screwdriver, "whips fixed pliant and slenderly recovering in their sockets" on buggies, factory smokestacks, shower-heads in hardware store windows, and cigar stubs, which he collects (TS, pp. 7, 44, 45, 46). As with Quentin Compson's obsessions in *The Sound and the Fury*, Faulkner displays Elmer's pre-adolescent sexuality through Freudian images.[8] In *The Interpretation of Dreams* (translated in 1913 by Freud's American disciple A. A. Brill) Freud had pointed out that sexual curiosity in growing youths took the form of an interest in the genitals of their own and the other sex and that any elongated object could serve as a symbol for the male organ. Faulkner's knowledge of Freud

---

[i-xix] for a series of unnumbered pages, the last of which seems to be non-sequential; 66-90, [91], 92-94; and 73x-106x, designating repeated numbering (i.e., 73-94) on pages that contain distinct material. "Elmer" is divided into Books I, II, and III; each Book is broken into many sections numbered in arabic. Material I designate 73x-106x was originally Book III, but was renumbered Book II. Page 72 ends Book I; pages 73-94 make up the original Book II, which has been renumbered III, although the pagination was not altered, except for the cancellation of page numbers 73 and 74. Unpublished Faulkner material quoted with the generous permission of Mrs. Jill Faulkner Summers.

    [8] The evidence of "Elmer" underlines the conclusion that poor Quentin never emerges from puberty in his preoccupations with phallic shapes. "Elmer" contains several preliminary sketches for Faulkner's later works. Jo-Addie prefigures Caddy, while her name suggests that of Addie Bundren; Elmer's father is not only Snopes-like, but also very much like Anse Bundren. Professor Meriwether has told me that among the Rowanoak papers is a short story entitled "As I Lay Dying" that is a version of the ending of the "Spotted Horses" material. There is startling evidence in Faulkner's early work that most of his characters and thematic preoccupations existed in his mind almost from the beginning of his writing career. Recall, for example, his statement that the Snopes material created "Wash," the story version of one of the climactic episodes of *Absalom, Absalom!* See *The Faulkner-Cowley File*, ed. Malcolm Cowley (New York: Viking, 1966), p. 26. "Elmer" leads forward to many Faulkner books, but the most surprising and most thorough connection is to *The Wild Palms* (1939).

comforting familiar spareness of her hip. He thrust his hands out
quickly, clutching.

    Yes, they had deserted him, and he wailed. Then
hands, woman's hands, came into his blind red loneliness and he
clung again to comforting ↑human↑ cloth, burrowing. The hands ca-
ressed him wrapping the skirt around his nakedness. It was not his
mother nor his sister: he knew that by the smell; but he smelt kind-
ness and clung closer, weeping. A voice said "He aint got a stitch
on, the little tyke" and another voice laughed with coarse uninten-
tional crudeness. "Hush, Lafe," the voice belonging to the hands
that held him xxix commanded and his back was patted through hasty
gingham. Clinging, shielded from the heat young Elmer wept for himself, for man, for all the sorrows of the race, seeing against his
tight eyelids his father hopping on one leg trying to don his pants
while light ran thinly in the hairs on his leg like a shallow grass-
   seeing
fire;/ that bitter-faced strange woman that ~~was once~~ *ought to be* his mother; his
howling brothers and his sister proud and tearless breathing fire
and flourishing on it like a salamander, growing away from him for
all time. So Elmer did not ~~see~~ *Remark* the loud excited volunteers inside
their
~~the~~/house throwing the things they had dragged for so long over the
face of the north half of the western world and that he loved: the
         rocked
low chair in which his mother/while he knelt in an impossible excru-
tiating rapture with his head in her lap; that dilapidated metal
box inscribed Bread in faded gold leaf in which he had kept for xxxix
a large part of his life a severed bird's wing, a basket carved cunningly from the seed of a peach, a thumbed lithograph of Joan of Arc

Illustration 1. "Elmer" TS, p. 6.

is still in dispute, but a recent survey of Freud's influence in America indicates that the psychoanalyst's ideas, particularly his ideas about dream interpretation, symbolism, and sex, were widely known, and disputed, in both medical and popular literature during the second and third decades of the twentieth century.[9] There can be little doubt that Faulkner's proliferated imagery puts a comic gloss on Elmer's sexual coming of age; the boy's fascinations are normal, if exaggerated, and his fixations actually play a major role in his becoming a particular kind of artist. As Kenneth Hepburn points out in his 1968 dissertation chapter on "Elmer," Elmer experiences a full range of sexual feelings before he is confirmed in heterosexuality and succumbs to the lure of romantic love with a woman.[10]

Elmer's relationship to his sister raises a hint of the theme of incest that recurs in later Faulkner works, but Jo-Addie tries to teach him that "You don't have to put your hands on folks to like 'em" (TS, p. 9). She gets into bed with him in the same angular way that Charlotte Rittenmeyer in *The Wild Palms* comes to her lover, all elbows and knees, angles and jabs (TS, p. 14; see *TWP*, p. 116). When Elmer is eleven, she leaves the family, disappearing from their lives completely and producing another trauma for the boy. His two brothers have gone already, one at Paris, Tennessee, to join a horse dealer "with a twenty-two ounce watch chain" (TS, p. 7) and the other at Memphis to strike out for St. Louis. The family moves westward and in Jonesboro, Arkansas, about sixty miles beyond Memphis, Jo-Addie departs, with no farewell except for sending Elmer a box of crayons a few days after her disap-

---

[9] See Nathan G. Hale, Jr., *Freud and the Americans: The Beginnings of Psychoanalysis in the United States, 1876-1917* (New York: Oxford University Press, 1971), pp. 290, 397-433. When he carried material from "Elmer" into *The Wild Palms,* whether by memory, by association with the sources of the earlier work, or by consultation of "Elmer," Faulkner kept the phallic symbolism. The determinant event of the book, an abortion, is prefigured in the first chapter where the middle-aged doctor descends a closed stairwell with his flashlight beam "lancing on before him" ([New York: Random House, 1939], p. 3). The tall convict loves his plow mule and cannot handle a gun. Androgyny and hermaphroditism are played upon in both plots of the novel (*TWP*, pp. 129, 242).

[10] Hepburn, "*Soldiers' Pay* to *The Sound and the Fury*: Development of Poetic in the Early Novels of William Faulkner," Ph.D. diss., University of Washington, 1968, p. 73.

pearance. Like Joe Christmas's life, Elmer's later career is
bound and controlled by his early experiences and the images
or objects which represent them. Art and sex are connected.
The phallic shapes of his tubes of paint and his desire to win
the love of fierce epicene Diana-like girls, through fame, retain
the same close association as the one which exists between his
childish fascination with cigar stubs and buggy whips and his
love of a thin adolescent sister. The importance of the color
red is involved in both sets of associations. Much is made of
the gift crayons; for a long time Elmer will not "deface their
pointed symmetrical purity" (TS, p. 18) and the red one stands
out vividly. The source of this gift, Jo-Addie, will pass across
his vision once more, but only fleetingly, and apparently as a
New Orleans prostitute. As for the family, "for all they knew
she might be Gloria Swanson or J. P. Morgan's wife" (TS, p.
30). The foreshadowing of Caddy Compson, even to the name,
is obvious.

In the fourth grade, Elmer "loves" a handsome schoolboy,
but that love is cruelly spurned when Elmer becomes the butt
of a schoolyard prank instigated by the beloved one.[11] He is
still undifferentiated sexually; for instance, he is deeply attached to a picture of Joan of Arc, though he has added a
mustache and an imperial jacket. (As the omniscient author
says, the English had made her a martyr, the French had made
her a saint, "it waited for Elmer Hodge to make [her] a man"
[TS, p. 7].) He is, however, gradually "getting to be a big
boy. Too big for his age" (TS, p. 45). Emerging from puberty,
he now draws smokestacks and armless people with phallic
shapes, and he has his first true experience with heterosexual
love. It is identified with a "full red mouth never quite completely closed" (TS, p. 47), an impression that stirs all his
complex feelings about red, about his brothers and sisters at
the fire, and about Jo-Addie. His ideal is a "Dianalike girl with

---

[11] Another boy in the class was "later to become a playwright of
renown" ["literary critic" was cancelled just before "playwright"]
(TS, p. 33), a possible reference to Stark Young, the drama critic,
novelist and playwright who, much older than Faulkner, had lived in
Oxford and had befriended the younger writer. The episode seems
to take place in Jonesboro, Arkansas, or Little Rock; both cities are
named and both deleted.

an impregnable integrity, a slimness virginal and impervious to time or circumstance" (TS, p. 47; see also pp. [iv], [xiv]).

By the time he is grown, Elmer's family is reduced to himself and his father; his mother has died and his father uses the insurance to buy a house in Texas, an ironic settlement, since the stricken woman, it is pointed out, had always wanted a home. The wanderer, who resembles Anse Bundren (he is too "lazy to get bald" [TS, p. 29]), will not leave his chair on the porch even when he needs a match to light his pipe; instead, he learns to chew the tobacco. The section ends with his making a gesture like Flem Snopes's at the end of *The Hamlet;* he spits into a barren flower-bed in the yard, a further irony against the memory of the mother, who had always wanted flowers but never stayed in one place long enough to cultivate them.

In manhood, Elmer becomes more involved with women and he goes to war. He has a "bastard son in Houston" (TS, p. 23), but the girl, Ethel, has sent him away when her pregnancy is evident. He joins the army. During grenade practice on the troop ship bound abroad, he throws a live hand grenade with his "awkward hands" (TS, p. 66); it bounces into a crowd of soldiers, killing one and wounding Elmer. He spends the rest of his service in a hospital. "War to him was not red. It was not even brown any longer" (TS, p. 67).[12] Recovered, except for a limp which causes him to use a cane, and demobilized with his back pay, Elmer goes in search of his family. After an idyll in New York and a fairly long sojourn in New Orleans— "voluptuous inertia mocking all briskness" (TS, p. 68)[13]—he

---

[12] Possibly an echo of Stephen Crane's *The Red Badge of Courage.* Crane is only one of the literary impressionists whose language is echoed in Faulkner's work. For early mention of Crane by Faulkner, see the article by Michael Millgate elsewhere in this issue, "Faulkner on the Literature of the First World War." It is worth noting that *The Wild Palms,* to which Faulkner carried so many things from "Elmer," is also sprinkled with echoes of Crane, notably in the "Old Man" sections where the "tall convict" and other nameless characters recall Crane's usual practice.

[13] Faulkner treats New Orleans much as Sherwood Anderson does in his 1925 novel, *Dark Laughter,* a book Anderson was working on when Faulkner was in New Orleans prior to his departure for Europe. Anderson's hero passes through the city, too, and he evokes it as "Song in the air, a slow dance" or "A broken jargon of words in the head" ([New York: Boni and Liveright, 1925], pp. 76, 78). For further

makes his way to Houston, where his father lives, and takes a job pumping gas in a service station. It has been five years since his affair with Ethel, but he thinks of her constantly, if unrealistically, in terms of the ideal: "a fierce proud Dianalike girl, small and dark and impregnably virginal" (TS, p. [iv]). Like the lovers in *The Wild Palms,* he feels they have been two against the world. He cannot believe that people could sin as they have "and then have nature, life, civilization . . . ignore it" (TS, p. [v]). The truth is, the world has not noticed. Ethel is married to a successful young businessman; she is ignorant of the meanings which Elmer attaches to their old affair. She and her husband happen into the gas station where Elmer works, the husband giving him "a soft cruel hand in that automatic celluloid sincerity cultivated by young successful business men" (TS, p. [viii]). The similarities to *The Wild Palms* are striking, including imagery that Faulkner elaborated in the "Old Man" section of his 1939 novel. Elmer sees them as "two partners in a beautiful intimate sin swept once more together, bearing calm and fearless the innocent rosy fruit of it in their joined arms" (TS, p. [v]). Harry Wilbourne (who also has bungling awkward hands; see *TWP,* p. 60) and Charlotte Rittenmeyer are likewise swept away by a passion, but the mode is serious and tragic, not comic, and they pay the price of their sin when they seek to abort the child their love has conceived. In a comic mode, the convict in the related sub-plot, "Old Man," is also swept away, literally, with a pregnant woman. Elmer sees his life as a tunnel; Harry sees himself on an unreturning stream (*TWP,* p. 34). Elmer dreams of meeting Ethel "across a threshold" and finds that her husband's house "breathed prosperity" (TS, p. [xvi]); the scene is like one in *The Wild Palms* where Harry bids what he thinks is a last goodbye to Charlotte across the threshold of her husband's middle-class home (TWP, pp. 42-43; see Illustration 2). The husband's handshake, described above, is like one which the man Bradley gives Harry in the later novel, "a brief hard violent bone-crushing meaningless grip—the broker's front man two years out of an Eastern college" (TWP, p. 106).

relationships between Faulkner's work and Anderson's, see my article, "Anderson, Hemingway, and Faulkner's *The Wild Palms,*" *PMLA,* 87 (May 1972), 465-74.

"Why . . .   if he's here." She was silent and motion-
less for a moment. Yes, of course. I'll go and see get him. Make
yourself at home," she added in that unnecessary pitch. "I'll bring
the baby down immediately. You'll wait here, wont you?"

"Of course," Elmer replied in a mild surprise. He did not v
even watch her as she crossed the room and mounted the stairs.

The child descended the stairs with a spoiled exasperating
slowness. Good Lord Elmer thought on realizing how big it was, realizing for the first time that he had expected a babe in arms. But it
was five years old and it crossed the room toward him a mature arro-
gance of detachment, staring at him. Elmer stared back at his son
in amazement. Its hair was of no particular shade at all, its eyes
were an opaque angry green, and it raised a petulant puffy face embry-
onic with that feminine sort of cruelty which ignores all masculine
standards of fair play. Its body beneath the fat of candy and ice
cream was firmly-poised and splendid; and in a devastating moment
Elmer had a vision of it grown, a man, with those opaque eyes and
that cruel face refined somewhat and attractive with a petulant at-
tractiveness, and a body splendid and lean as his was once preying on
women of all classes, probably diseased and spreading disease with
glee. It dropped the ball it carried, and wept: its mother recovered it with a careful xxxxxxxxxxxxxxxxxxxxxxxxxxxxxxxxxxxxxxxxxx
and conscious grace to which temporary abnegation of self lent a sort
of splendor. The child dropped the ball again immediately. It rolled
under Elmer's chair and the child followed it and stood staring at
Elmer, the ball forgotten, kicking his ankle rythmically. Elmer
said: " You keep a maid all day now, dont you?"

The child screamed, tearless above its gaping mouth, watching
him with the blankness of a carven idol. "Want your ball?" he said

Elmer tells Ethel, "I'm going to be a painter," and then he has to explain that he means "paint pictures" instead of houses (TS, p. [xvii]), the same statement and explanation made by Harry to the middle-aged doctor in the first chapter of *The Wild Palms*. The actual moment Elmer decides to become an artist is not given explicitly, though *this* may be the moment. His decision seems related to his desire for Ethel. Later passages indicate that he has adopted art as a vocation in part, at least, as a means to fame, and fame as the agency to win the girl he wants, though by the time these revelations come the girl will not be Ethel but Myrtle Monson. He is, however, apparently serious (unlike Harry Wilbourne, who has proved to be colorblind); and his career is possible because he has lost his dread of the color red:

> There was a picture in the Hutchinson galleries that had red in it, that for Elmer was all red. It was by a Frenchman and it may have been a vase of flowers or a woman's dress: he had forgotten which; but from it he had learned that no color has any value, any significance save in its relation to other colors seen or suggested or imagined. (TS, p. 28)

This discovery in the Chicago Art Institute gallery, which is apparently a Faulkner fabrication, since the gallery did not exhibit modern works,[14] has a good deal of importance for Faulkner's art as well as Elmer's, and it may provide a key to the understanding of Faulkner's early experiments with

---

14 Faulkner's reference is a fabrication in the sense that the Hutchinson Gallery in Chicago's Art Institute did not exhibit modern painting, to which the example seems to refer, but the old masters, particularly Dutch and Flemish. It may be significant, in the context, that in "Portrait of Elmer" there is a passage where the young man is "thinking of Hals and Rembrandt" (TS, p. 50), whose work was in the Hutchinson Gallery, apparently hung side by side (according to a May 1922 *Handbook of Paintings and Drawings* from the Art Institute). The Hutchinson Gallery, however, was decorated in red, and among the other collections at the Institute in the 1920's were some late 19th and early 20th-century French paintings, as well as related works. There was one work by Sherwood Anderson's brother, Karl. The only title in the 1922 *Handbook* that immediately appears to bear on Faulkner's reference is a painting by a "contemporary" Frenchman name Jean Puy entitled "Woman in Red." One wonders if Faulkner were drawing on the report of someone like Anderson and if the reference might not go back to 1913 and the famous Armory Show of modernist paintings. Information about the Hutchinson, and the *Handbook*, supplied by Cecilia Chin, Reference Librarian, Art Institute of Chicago, May 3, 1973.

narrative technique, including the structure of "Elmer." Leaving the discussion of this for later, however, the point to be observed here is that Elmer is confirmed as an artist. Now there is only the need for time, a letting up of necessity, so he can paint (TS, p. [xiv]). The same language will recur in an ironic context at the end of "Portrait of Elmer," where the young man's story progresses farther than it does in the unfinished novel. In "Elmer," he continues to fantasize the possibility of taking up where he left off with Ethel; the tone of the novel becomes deadly serious, if a little melodramatic. At this point the novel breaks off abruptly at the conclusion of a scene between Elmer, Ethel, and their child. Elmer stares at his son "in amazement," and the child's screams end the section.

Another girl enters the novel. Her name is Myrtle Monson—apparently once "Mooney," to judge from a strikeover on TS p. 25; both names associate her with Elmer's Dianalike dream girl and with his aspirations in art. She is "like a star, clean and unattainable for all her—Henry James would have called it vulgarity—humanness" (TS, p. 23). Though this too is not specified in the novel as we have it, Myrtle is now abroad possibly because her mother has wanted to take her away from Elmer, who, as a gas station attendant, has no prospects. The Monsons are rich, perhaps newly rich: "in the year 1921 . . . Myrtle's old man got himself involved in another oil well; and in 1922 Myrtle and her mother went to Europe" (TS, p. 24). Although his feelings about her remain mixed—"God. He did not want Myrtle now as wife or sweetheart" (TS, p. [xix])—Elmer is on a freighter bound for Europe, apparently determined to begin the study of painting that will make him famous and help him win his girl.

This shipboard scene is the actual opening of Faulkner's novel, and from it, as a present moment, Elmer's past is revealed through numerous flashbacks. Looking a little like a Snopes in his Sunday best, Elmer wears "tennis shoes and a stiff-brimmed straw hat" (TS, p. 3). He nurses a "varnished yellow stick" as a result of his war wound. He has brought "Clive Bell," possibly Bell's 1922 volume *Since Cezanne*;[15] Élie Faure's *Out-*

---

[15] Anderson knew the book; possibly he owned a copy. He had sent one to his artist brother Karl in August 1922. *Letters of Sherwood Anderson*, ed. Walter B. Rideout and H. M. Jones (Boston: Little,

line of Art;[16] and six saccharine American novels. But he doesn't read, or paint, on the voyage, though he also owns an expensive set of paints. The tubes of oil call up the childhood memories rehearsed above. He likes to "finger lasciviously smooth dull silver tubes virgin yet at the same time pregnant . . . innocent clean brushes . . . chubby bottles of oil" (TS, p. 3). There is a kind of aesthetic masturbation here akin to Elmer's love of impregnable, virginal epicene women.[17] The passage seems to signify the impotence, or sterility, of the too-ideal, whether it is in art or life, a theme that Faulkner touched throughout his career as a novelist. Elmer anticipates being an artist instead of practicing his craft. In these "fat portentous tubes . . . was yet wombed his heart's desire, the world itself— thickbodied and female and at the same time phallic; hermaphroditic" (TS, p. 4).[18] The fore part of the ship is "graceful as the unconfined body of a dancing girl" (TS, p. 20), but there

---

Brown, 1953), p. 88. Possibly through Gertrude Stein, Anderson was also interested in Cézanne; in another letter he notifies a friend that "David Prall finally got the Cezanne prints," apparently something Anderson had arranged for his brother-in-law. Prall was a professor of aesthetics (Harvard 1920-21; University of California, 1921-30, etc.) and brother to Anderson's third wife, Elizabeth. Prall is also probably the indirect agent of Faulkner's knowing Anderson, since Prall and Stark Young (see fn. 11, above) became friends at the University of Texas in 1912-15, and in 1920 Young helped Faulkner get a job in the New York bookstore which the then-Miss Prall managed (see Millgate, *Achievement,* p. 9). This set up the relationship from which Faulkner benefited in New Orleans in 1924-25. Millgate. *Achievement,* pp. 16-17; Anderson, *Letters,* p. 167. Another possible reference is Bell's 1913 *Art* (New York: Frederick Stokes), which has a good deal on post-Impressionism and Cézanne's influence.

16 One of the books Phil Stone ordered in the early twenties, when Faulkner was reading widely from Stone's library, was Élie Faure's *History of Art.* Joseph Blotner, comp., *William Faulkner's Library: A Catalogue* (Charlottesville: University of Virginia Press, 1964), p. 124.

17 Compare, by way of explanation, and as an example of another remarkable resonance of "Elmer" in *The Wild Palms,* Harry Wilbourne's attitude toward money and his fondling the $300 check "Rat" Rittenmeyer has given for Charlotte's passage home: "this was a form of masturbation (thinking, *because I am still, and probably will always be, in the puberty of money)*" (*TWP,* p. 94).

18 In *The Wild Palms,* the imagery is transferred to the cans of food which, like the check above, become another symbol of time and money for Harry: "the dynamic torpedolike solid shapes" (*TWP,* p. 114). Closer still to the later imagery is the description of the tubes of paint in "Portrait of Elmer": "The tubes lay in serried immaculate rows, blunt, solid, torpedolike, latent" (PoE, p. 50). For the hermaphroditism, see fn. 9 above.

is also "time enough for myrtle" (TS, p. [xix]; the lower case is Faulkner's and perhaps intentional, playing on the association of "myrtle," like laurel, with fame). He wavers between success in art and success with women, and he has a vision of himself as "Elmer Hodge the painter," thinking simultaneously of "the bodies of girls soon to be old and wrinkled but now troubling and sweet as music [undecipherable word] articulate beneath the year turning reluctant as a young bride to the old lean body of death"[19] (TS, p. [xix]).

With Elmer arrived in Italy, where Venice is "spired like voluptuous lace," Faulkner indulges in a little Joycean word-play and has Elmer come up with the free association, "How like *lice* we really are" (TS, p. 74; my italics). He is apparently now rich, a fact omitted heretofore and not explained, though Faulkner probably intended to explain it in the finished book. "Portrait of Elmer" reveals that Elmer's shiftless father's property has produced oil. With some of the ship's crew, and in the company of a Venetian whore—"Clean no odor diana"—he goes to a bar. The glass from which he drinks is "phallic," the evening is riotous, and after a decadent fantasy of the streets something like the nighttown episode of *Ulysses,* Elmer finds himself in jail because he has put his foot on a piece of Italian money, abusing the king's countenance and thereby committing treason. The episode, based on something that really happened to Faulk-ner's companion on the European trip, Bill Spratling,[20] is the source for the story "Divorce in Naples." Angelo Marina, a young Italian also in jail, gets out and takes a message to Elmer's shipmates, who bail him out. He leaves Venice in Angelo's company. Paris—where, the second officer of the ship has told him, "you can see the Louver"—is

> that homely informal garden where the ghost of George Moore's dead life wanders politely in a pale eroticism;—all of that merry childish sophisticated cold-blooded dying city to which Cezanne was dragged by his friends like a reluctant cow, where Degas and Manet fought obscure points of color and line and love, cursing Bougereau and his curved pink female flesh, where Matisse and

---

[19] The passage is similar to the ending of "Portrait of Elmer" and that, in turn, closely resembles the ending of *Sanctuary.* See fn. 49, below.

[20] *File on Spratling,* pp. 32-33.

Picasso yet painted. (TS, p. [xix], an uncontinuous page following
p. [xviii])

The language of the symbolists, like "insincere guitar," and the
color sense of the Impressionists, like "Gamboge" (a strong
yellow), is there (TS, p. 19). Like Quentin Compson, Elmer
meditates on time, aware that it goes on ceaselessly despite him
(TS, pp. 28-29). He wonders if "it made any difference where
you went: that you wanted certain things and you either got
them or you didn't, but if you wanted them hard enough you
usually did" (TS, p. 20), a passage strongly like some of Charlotte Rittenmeyer's pronouncements in *The Wild Palms*. But
these are thoughts in anticipation; this section of the novel
breaks off before the young men reach Paris.

Both sections of the novel dealing specifically with Elmer
himself seem to break off incomplete. They were originally
Books I and II, while the original Book III is devoted to the
Monsons, mother and daughter, and related matters. At some
point in the book's history, Faulkner renumbered the Monson
material and made it Book II, putting it where it would divide
the two books about Elmer. The expedient seems a late strategy,
and desperate, but Faulkner's problems were more acute than
these repairs could correct. Even as it stands, the segment
devoted to the Monsons is incomplete and seriously flawed,
particularly in the last several sections where Faulkner introduces
a new set of characters. This book of "Elmer" follows Myrtle
and her mother during their trip to Europe and their three-year
sojourn abroad, though not in great detail. About Myrtle we
learn chiefly that she is flirtatious, fickle, and getting fat. The
last point is of some importance; Elmer had noted that Ethel
was getting fat, too. The idea is not elaborated, but the attention
to the developing figures of these young ladies satirizes the
artist's need and preference for the epicene boy-girls of his
youthful dreams; in a word, it also predicts the true course of
romantic love. Mrs. Monson, a mild American puritan, learns
to drink wine; she does it religiously and without pleasure. She
tries to enter European society. Given the earlier reference to
Henry James, there seems to be a bit of Daisy Millerism going
on here, but with a heavier hand than the Master's. After our
introduction to the Monsons come nine poor sections that con-

cern a family of down-and-out English aristocrats who hope to repair their fortunes by marrying the Monsons, mother and daughter. The humor is weak; the characterization flimsy. This book of the novel ends, or trails off, with a return to Mrs. Monson's viewpoint as she tries to persuade her bored daughter to have tea with the Englishmen.

How Faulkner might have united, or ended, the three elements of his plot is not clear, especially as one considers the nine sections of Book III (or II, as it was re-cast) which seem so unpromising. The structure he was apparently working toward is the kind of juxtaposition he employs successfully in the Benbow-Sartoris relationship in "Flags in the Dust" (a balance somewhat damaged when Ben Wasson cut that novel down to make *Sartoris*[21]) and, even more successfully, in the Lena Grove, Byron Bunch, Gail Hightower, Joe Christmas, Joanna Burden plots of *Light in August*. His failure in "Elmer," as Michael Millgate has suggested, may have resulted in part from the use of autobiographical sources which he did not control with proper aesthetic distance.[22] Powerful unassimilated feelings do rise through the surface fiction of "Elmer," invariably violating the tone and comic purpose of the book. Still, what seems to have spelled the doom of "Elmer" is the attention to the English upper class, at the opposite pole, one would suppose, from any autobiographical elements in the novel. Faulkner would abandon only these scenes when he reworked parts of the novel into stories later on, while he was able to bring the

---

[21] See Millgate, *Achievement*, p. 82.

[22] Millgate, p. 22. Hepburn, in his dissertation, naively disputes Millgate's remarks about autobiography in "Elmer," saying that it cannot be autobiographical because the Falkners were not inveterate movers and that Faulkner did not have a sister. The Falkners did in fact move a lot: from New Albany to Ripley to Oxford and numerous times within Oxford. Faulkner did not have a sister, but a cousin, Sallie Murry Wilkins, now Mrs. R. X. Williams of Oxford, was raised with the Falkner boys. See accounts of family life by the brothers John (*My Brother Bill*, 1963) and Murry (*The Falkners of Mississippi*, 1967), and the pictures on pp. 146 and 148 of Martin Dain's *Faulkner's County* (New York: Random House, 1964), which show Sallie Murry and the Falkner boys. One may speculate that Ethel and Myrtle may owe something to two of Faulkner's early sweethearts, Estelle Oldham and Helen Baird, and that Faulkner is also drawing on Spratling's youth. See Millgate, pp. 3, 6; "Anderson, Hemingway and Faulkner's *The Wild Palms*;" and *File on Spratling*, pp. 3-6.

personal material under control in such novels as *The Sound and the Fury* and *The Wild Palms.*

For all the rough similarities between the two books, "Elmer" is a great deal less interesting than its predecessor, *Soldiers' Pay,* although it seems intended to mark a step beyond the first novel. In "Elmer," Faulkner was experimenting more boldly with narrative technique, with shifts in time and free association, with an awareness of Freud and Joyce, and also, perhaps, he was attempting to translate the innovations of the Impressionist and post-Impressionist painters into literary form, as Gertrude Stein and Sherwood Anderson had done and as Ernest Hemingway was currently doing. The book which follows is *Mosquitoes* (1927), written in Pascagoula, Mississippi, near New Orleans, after his return from Europe. "Elmer" and *Mosquitoes* are very much akin; still experimenting with style and structure, Faulkner also again draws upon recent personal experience and once more takes up the problems of art and the artist. There are many literal borrowings from "Elmer," as, for instance, the long passages describing the movements of the three soft-footed priests and their encounter with the dead beggar.[23] Faulkner has less trouble with the form of the next book, and perhaps it is because he found in the yacht trip at the center of the novel a convenient structural device to bring all his characters together, but *Mosquitoes* is still far from being a great novel. Faulkner's genius became increasingly manifest in *Sartoris* and bloomed in *The Sound and the Fury* and *As I Lay Dying,* which all three show a family resemblance to "Elmer," not only because they borrow or translate characters, names, descriptions, and images, but also because they seem to represent a better working out of the narrative form Faulkner had attempted in the unfinished 1925 novel. Especially important, it seems to me, is the influence of modern painting and of Henri Bergson's concepts of time and memory (which themselves influenced the perceptions of the modern painters).

As Elmer Hodge's childhood is revealed through flashbacks we see him entering and emerging from puberty, buffeted by the experiences that socialize the child into the more or less normal adult. His childhood is dominated by powerful mem-

---

[23] *Mosquitoes* (New York: Boni and Liveright, 1927), pp. 335-38.

ories which lead eventually to his decision to become an artist, a decision reinforced by adult experiences like the war and his relations with women. The process is subtle and convincing; the result, given the imagery, seems inevitable. It is quite un- like what Thomas Wolfe would do in *Look Homeward, Angel* (1929) where, it has always seemed to me, the lack of selectivity in presenting Eugene Gant's experiences could justify making him an ax murderer or an evangelist or any number of things, except that Wolfe has resolved to depict the emergence of a literary genius and decrees the outcome. In "Elmer" the out- come seems decreed by the experience, which Faulkner has intuited brilliantly, for all his problems of execution; it is Faulkner's careful choice and deployment of his materials that makes it convincing, a strategy, I would like to suggest, which seems to rest on a theory of memory very like Bergson's and a presentation closely related to the devices of post-Impressionist painting.

The novel begins in a fictional present, but in hiatus. Elmer is on the boat bound for Europe. On the first page of the typescript he reflects on the isolation he has enjoyed during the voyage; it has given him "a sense of firmness, of independence, as if solitude had . . . welded him into a compact erectness" (TS, p. 1). Approaching land, he feels human again, remembering what "circumstance and his fellow man could do to him." This is the context in which Elmer's childhood is revealed, an opening which seems to announce that he has sorted out his experiences and come to a temporary sense of himself. Who and what he is, then, is clarified from this point by the flashbacks.

Kenneth Hepburn has argued in his dissertation that Elmer's ruminations on the past are destructive of his art, that he needs solitude like that on the ship to achieve the proper aesthetic posture or mood, which Hepburn equates with Elmer's phrase, "compact erectness." Hepburn sees "Elmer" as a "novel about the production of a work of art" where the major effort is "an attempt to arrive at more or less simultaneous definitions of art and of the artist."[24] The handling of time in the novel is most important, according to Hepburn. Faulkner "seems to

---

[24] Hepburn, p. 68.

be attempting to define . . . a proper working relationship among time, memory, and art." In "Elmer," he writes, there "is a complex oscillation through time by which the present, as partially made manifest through memory, is described as the proper locus out of which art might flow."[25] Elmer needs to free himself from the past and what it represents in order to paint, according to Hepburn; when he leaves the ship and enters time again, however, he will again be the victim of more examples of what "circumstance and his fellow man" can do to him, and he will be distracted from pursuing his goal of becoming an artist.

Hepburn seems aware that artists are apparently made, and not always born, and that circumstance and his fellow man actually have determined Elmer to be a painter in the first place, but he believes that Elmer "is reliving past presents to the detriment of his art which demands a coalesced present out of which to operate."[26] The difficulty here derives from the manner in which Hepburn represents Faulkner's conception of time. Hepburn sees these memories, these "past presents," as he calls them, as "almost discrete quanta" of time and not as part of a continuum,[27] but the contrary is true. Whether or not Faulkner was consciously or deeply aware of Henri Bergson's philosophy at this time in his life—he did say much later that his notion of time was Bergsonian[28]—the concept of time and memory in "Elmer" is closer to Bergson's theories than it is to Hepburn's notion. If it is not skillfully handled, as it is in *The Sound and the Fury,* for instance, it is nevertheless rather clearly present. In *An Introduction to Metaphysics,* a relatively simple statement of his philosophy that was conveniently translated into English in 1912 by T. S. Eliot's friend T. E. Hulme, Bergson discusses the one reality which we can all know, "our self which endures," in terms appropriate to "Elmer." The following passage is quoted at length because of its suggestiveness for the novel under consideration as well as for other Faulkner works:

---

[25] Hepburn, p. 70.
[26] Hepburn, p. 70.
[27] Hepburn, p. 68.
[28] *Lion in the Garden,* p. 70.

When I direct my attention inward to contemplate my own self (supposed for the moment to be inactive), I perceive at first, as a crust solidified on the surface, all the perceptions which come to it from the material world. These perceptions are clear, distinct, juxtaposed or juxtaposable one with another; they tend to group themselves into objects. Next, I notice the memories which more or less adhere to these perceptions and which serve to interpret them. These memories have been detached, as it were, from the depth of my personality, drawn to the surface by the perceptions which resemble them. . . . Lastly, I feel the stir of tendencies and motor habits—a crowd of virtual actions, more or less firmly bound to these perceptions and memories.[29]

Beneath this surface, Bergson goes on, is a "continuous flux," a "succession of states" that can "only be said to form multiple states when I have already passed them and turn back to observe their track. Whilst I was experiencing them they were so solidly organized, so profoundly animated with a common life, that I could not have said where any one of them finished or where another commenced. In reality no one of them begins or ends, but all extend into each other."[30] "This inner life," Bergson says, "may be compared to the unrolling of a coil" or "to a continual rolling up, like that of a thread on a ball, for our past follows us, it swells incessantly with the present that it picks up on its way; and consciousness means memory."[31]

Distrustful of all images or words, however, Bergson goes on to say that no metaphor can express the "development of self in duration" accurately. This must be known by intuition, although metaphysics can pile up many diverse images which may, "by the convergence of their action, direct consciousness to the precise point where there is a certain intuition to be seized." Such an idea is, in essence, the source for the tech-

---

[29] Henri Bergson, *Introduction to Metaphysics,* trans. T. E. Hulme (New York: G. P. Putnam's Sons, 1912), p. 25.

[30] *Ibid.*

[31] Bergson, pp. 25-26. The thread-spool imagery seems to recur in *Sartoris* (New York: Harcourt, Brace, 1929), p. 357: "As though her life were closing, not into the future, but out of the past, like a spool being rewound"; in *As I Lay Dying* (1930), corrected ed. (New York: Random House, 1964), pp. 139, "time . . . runs parallel between us like a looping string," and 198, "If you could just ravel out into time"; and in *Light in August* (New York: Smith & Haas, 1932), p. 6: "sight and sense drowsily merge and blend, like the road itself, with all the peaceful and monotonous changes between darkness and day, like already measured thread being rewound onto a spool."

niques of the post-Impressionist painters as well as for Eliot's concept of the "objective correlative." A single concept, like a single representation in painting, is a symbol substituted for the object it symbolizes, demanding no effort and holding only "that part of an object which is common to it." It constitutes a comparison, and a partial one at that. But setting concept by concept, or metaphor by metaphor, we reconstruct the whole object and its parts, according to Bergson, through suggestion.[32] Eliot's poetry is an example of the process; the paintings of the post-Impressionists are another, wherein they attempted to represent reality by the accumulation of images, patches or points of color, or by a series of canvases which showed a scene in different lights during different times of the day or year.

The whole of "Elmer" Book I as we have it occurs on shipboard where Elmer is in a kind of momentary "suspension"; in the Bergsonian sense he is inactive and able to contemplate his own self. He has a number of present visual experiences: the prow of the ship like a young girl, the red-throated ventilators which the captain of the ship uses in his model building, his own books and paints and the varnished cane. These form the "crust" of perceptions from the material world. Then there are the memories which adhere to these perceptions: the color red brings up the fire, the gift crayons, his first encounter with sex, the "red horror" of his "war" experience, the picture in the Chicago art gallery that frees him from his trauma. These associations are complexly involved with certain women: his mother, Jo-Addie, Ethel, Myrtle; the women in turn have also had something to do with his becoming an artist. There is more, but the point is, as Bergson would say, that we cannot know ourselves—or know any other thing—except through intuition, but using appropriate concepts and images we can achieve a representation that focuses intuition or causes it to occur. The process is not literal, but suggestive, approximate, but, finally, if enough images are used, approximate in an infinitely close way, somewhat like getting a "real" answer by using the infinite calculus. We may speak of this technique having two purposes in Faulkner's novel: it is a fictional strategy that orders the revelation of the story, and it is a representation of Elmer's

---

[32] Bergson, pp. 27-28.

own coming to consciousness of himself, the "self which endures." It is appropriate that one of Elmer's discoveries is to become "aware of time going ceaselessly on like a clock despite him" (TS, pp. 28-29).

Elmer will leave the ship and become involved with the Italian police, with his new servant Angelo, and finally with the reappearing Myrtle, and all these things will distract him from getting on with his work, but at the same time, if his past means anything, such things represent new experiences, new mutations of his memory, an altered consciousness, and thus new resources for understanding himself and his life and for creating art. No man can have solitude always; nor can any man bear too much of it and live, Faulkner says later in *The Wild Palms* (p. 138).

This is a comic satirical novel, and if we may judge by "Portrait of Elmer," which is to be discussed shortly, the young man is not going to be too successful. But, Hepburn to the contrary, there is a good deal of autobiography in "Elmer," as Millgate has suggested (see fn. 22), and that fact may help explain what is going on. Faulkner was always capable of giving himself a satirical thrust. Elmer's distractions and a number of Elmer's memories are the young Faulkner's, however transmuted, and, if anything, the experiences which produced them were probably more acute and painful to the sensitive young poet and novelist than the fictionalized problems become to his comical creation. Faulkner's childhood sweetheart, Estelle Oldham, had married and gone away; he himself left Oxford after her engagement, lived for a time with his friend Phil Stone in New Haven, and joined the Royal Air Force shortly after her marriage. Faulkner's "war wound" is still a matter of conjecture, though it is known that he did not fly officially or experience combat, but he did have a limp and a stick, like Elmer. He had a girl friend in Pascagoula and New Orleans, who may have been in Europe when he took his 1925 trip, and he would dedicate *Mosquitoes* to her, although the very day the book appeared her engagement to another man was announced in the New Orleans newspapers.[33] This list of ex-

---

[33] Millgate, *Achievement,* p. 6; New Orleans *Times-Picayune,* 1 May 1927, Sect. III, p. 4.

periences will doubtless be capable of expansion when a full biography appears, but the point to be made is that Faulkner controlled his memories, he fought off the distractions and temptations to which all would-be artists are inclined, and he created more than a few truly great works of art. Faulkner's memories were not detrimental to his art, even when they were apparently painful ones; they were both inspiration and resource material for his fiction. If Faulkner gives Elmer similar memories and distractions, therefore, he would not seem to be saying, as Hepburn argues, that reliving the past is of necessity detrimental to art, although in "Elmer" the main character is observed doing more recollecting than creating. There was, of course, the technical problem of telling Elmer's story, which demanded the flashbacks. They reveal that experience has *gradually* shaped the young American into a would-be artist. If he has trouble working now, perhaps he is still developing; if he continues to have trouble, that is paradox. There does come a moment when nothing will do except work, as Faulkner well knew, but putting together the unique shapes of one's own experience is a beginning and not a substitute for art. The next step involves finding the best formal representation for those elements, and that is also an important aspect of Faulkner's "Elmer."

In the New Orleans sketch, "Out of Nazareth," published April 12, 1925, Faulkner writes, "I remarked to Spratling [the young man who was also to be his companion to Europe] how no one since Cezanne had really dipped his brush in light. Spratling, whose hand has been shaped to a brush as mine has (alas!) not, here became discursive on the subject of transferring light to canvas."[34] Faulkner was apparently well aware of currents in modern painting, and it may be that this awareness also finds expression in "Elmer." Cézanne, particularly, whom Faulkner invokes in the novel, offers several possibilities. There are many conceivable lines of transmission—Spratling, the fact that Faulkner apparently knew Élie Faure's books

34 *William Faulkner: New Orleans Sketches,* ed. Carvel Collins, revised edition (New York: Random House, 1968), p. 46. In his revised introduction, Collins notes that Faulkner had not only done the now well-known drawings for student publications at the University of Mississippi, but that he had shown a "good sense of color in the paintings which illustrate his unpublished *Mayday*" (p. xxiii).

on modern art and Clive Bell's *Since Cezanne,* that in Paris he lived near the Luxembourg Gallery where works by Impressionists and post-Impressionists were displayed. But Sherwood Anderson and Gertrude Stein represent particularly interesting sources. Anderson's brother Karl was a professional painter, working in the manner of the Impressionists; Anderson himself painted; and Anderson knew Gertrude Stein and her work, which reflected the cross-fertilization of the graphic and literary arts. Anderson himself experimented with the techniques of the painters in his writing. Under Stein's influence, Hemingway was in Spain trying "to do the country like Cézanne."[35] Until Cézanne, Stein has said, a painting was composed around a central idea and all other elements were subordinated to that idea; but Cézanne conceived "that in composition one thing was as important as another thing." In *Three Lives* (1909), she said, she had tried to "convey the idea of each part of a composition being as important as the whole . . . [because in her view] one human being is as important as another . . . a blade of grass has the same value as a tree. . . . I was not interested in making the people real but in the essence or, as a painter would call it, value."[36]

Elmer, and Faulkner, knew something about "value" in the painter's sense, too, as a passage already quoted reveals. "It was in Chicago that he had lost his dread of the color red," learning from the French painting (apparently conceived as impressionistic) "that no color has any value, any significance save in its relation to other colors seen or suggested or

---

[35] *The Flowers of Friendship: Letters Written to Gertrude Stein,* ed. Donald Gallup (New York: Knopf, 1953), p. 164. Hemingway's letter is dated 16 August 1924. A discussion of Hemingway and the painters, among whom Cézanne is predominant, is in Emily Stipes Watts, *Ernest Hemingway and the Arts* (Urbana: University of Illinois Press, 1971).

[36] These remarks were recorded in a 1946 interview, printed in *A Primer for the Gradual Understanding of Gertrude Stein,* ed. R. B. Haas (Los Angeles: Black Sparrow Press, 1971), pp. 15-17. I have seen no evidence that Faulkner knew Stein's work, but he might have seen it, as well as heard from Anderson about it. Her influence, and the influence of Cézanne, were well known. In his autobiography, the poet William Carlos Williams who took a trip abroad the year before Faulkner, records that "It was the work of the painters following Cezanne and the Impressionists that, critically, opened up the age of Stein, Joyce and a good many others." *The Autobiography of William Carlos Williams* (New York: New Directions, 1951), p. 380.

imagined" (TS, p. 28). In "Elmer," a red crayon is as important as first sex experience or the war wound and none have value except in the complex relationship that produces Elmer Hodge the artist. One is reminded of William Carlos Williams' poem,

so much depends
upon

a red wheel
barrow

glazed with rain
water

beside the white
chickens[37]

—a poem where there is the same kind of juxtaposition as in Faulkner's fiction. In Faulkner's work, "so much depends" upon characters and events and images thrown into startling juxtaposition. It is worth noting that, by coincidence, The Four Seas Company of Boston, which published Faulkner's *The Marble Faun* in 1924, had brought out Stein's *Geography and Plays* (with an introduction by Anderson) in 1922 and Williams' *Kora in Hell* in 1920, both books impressionistic melanges in poetry and prose.

Many critics have complained that Faulkner's first novel, *Soldiers' Pay*, seems to be a novel without a central character or a single plot. Kenneth Hepburn, who offers a convenient summary of these views, goes on to say that it is a novel in which many characters can be central in what are, given different interpretations, many possible novels (Hepburn, p. 27). He assumes that Faulkner was at fault, unable to commit himself to writing anything less than an ideal novel. But in the context of Stein's experiments and theories, modelled as she said on Cézanne, Faulkner's use of character in *Soldiers' Pay* may have justifiable purpose, however unsatisfactory the result is aesthetically. It may be, as Hepburn thinks, that "any of a number of the possible frame tales could validly be postulated" as the principal frame tale, with a hero and a coherent

---

[37] Poem XXI from *Spring and All* (1923), taken from *The Complete Collected Poems of William Carlos Williams, 1906-1938* (Norfolk, Conn.: New Directions, 1938), p. 127.

reading for each and any, but it is also possible, as he does not
say, that the many elements are not frames at all but equal
parts juxtaposed, and that they make up a whole which constitutes a post-Impressionistic novel of the generation after the
war. There are other examples among Faulkner's early work
which seem to employ a similar technique. In *The Sound and
the Fury* (where each character incidentally may be said to
demonstrate a different naivete about the true nature of Bergson's concept of time[38]) the four sections create a portrait of
the absent Caddy and tell why she is absent and what her
absence means in the lives of those remaining. *As I Lay Dying*
is almost pointillist, with its fifty-nine stream-of-consciousness
passages; once again the absent figure, Addie, manages to occupy the foreground of the action.[39] *Light in August* is an excel-
lent extension of the technique of *Soldiers' Pay*. The title is
suggestive of the post-Impressionist consciousness of mutations
of reality produced by the quality of light during different times
of the day or year. The novel juxtaposes the lives of a number
of independent characters, all of them of major proportions, all
of them outsiders in the community where their lives briefly
intertwine, to create a whole impression.[40] The juxtaposed plots
of *The Wild Palms* create a whole by similar means.

"Elmer" is by no means the source of all Faulkner's early
fictional ideas,[41] but it should be apparent from the speculations
above that the unfinished novel was ambitious if ill-fated and
that in it Faulkner seems to be toying openly with ideas and

---

[38] Benjy is almost totally without consciousness of duration, a harp
upon whose strings the flow of time and memory plays a repetitive,
disordered tune; Quentin dwells in the past and seeks to stop time;
Jason rejects the past and looks to a future that Miss Quentin steals
from him; and Dilsey has the Christian belief in a beginning and an
ending to history, centered on the Christ event.

[39] The coffin upon the sawhorses is seen by Darl (who has been to
France in the army) as "like a cubistic bug" (*AILD,* corrected edition,
p. 209).

[40] Christmas and Hightower are studies in time consciousness, both
at odds with a true intuition of duration, Joe particularly a victim of
a few major images out of his past, while Lena Grove seems like a
personification of Bergsonian time, moving along her apparently endless road, accumulating, adapting. It is appropriate that the thread-
spool image noted above, fn. 31, occurs in the context of Lena's travelling.

[41] Crane has been mentioned; Conrad is another. Oldenburg, in
addition, suggests Norman Douglas and Ford Madox Ford.

techniques which he would perfect and couple with better material as his artistry matured. Where "Elmer" was headed is really impossible to judge from the unfinished typescript; perhaps, in the Bergsonian sense, the hero was striving toward a full creativity at the urging of the *élan vital*. He has overcome his traumatic fear of red; he has quashed his incestuous feelings for Jo-Addie; he has outgrown his love of the cruel and beautiful young man. He has fastened on two young women, one of whom he has given a child; he has suffered in the war; he has chosen art. But in the satirical context, one ought not to expect great success for him. Something like the wry and inconclusive ending of *Mosquitoes* may be what Faulkner had in mind. Exercising proper caution, we might consider the evidence of "Portrait of Elmer" as an aid to guessing Faulkner's intention in the novel upon which the story is loosely based.

The title "Portrait of Elmer Hodge" which exists on some miscellaneous papers collected with the "Elmer" typescript has caused some critical confusion in the past because the title was quite naturally identified as a new working title for the novel; the few pages of the treatment were taken as a new beginning, and they may be, though the approach is like that in "Portrait of Elmer," the later story version. Without further close examination of these papers and the papers recently found at Rowanoak, it is impossible to date all the material, but in both collections, it would seem, the 1925 work is mingled with work done in the 1930's. Thanks to Mr. Linton Massey, the Faulkner collector who acquired the full typescript of "Portrait of Elmer" and put it with the Faulkner papers at Virginia, we have a somewhat clearer view of the matter. Piecing the circumstances together from scant information, one can surmise that Faulkner wrote "Portrait of Elmer" in the early 1930's and submitted it, perhaps upon request, to Bennett Cerf at Random House. Among the papers at Virginia are some letters which seem to touch the matter indirectly. Faulkner writes his agent, Morton Goldman, in December 1931, to say that a new novel is going well (apparently *Light in August*), that he wants a contract with Hollywood soon, and that he will agree to whatever "Bennet" [Bennett Cerf] wants regarding the Elmer story. The nature of Cerf's interest or plans is unknown to me at present; per-

haps it was a limited edition like *Idyll in the Desert,* a long
Faulkner story which Random House had published in 1931.
With the "Portrait of Elmer" typescript at Virginia is a letter
from Philip C. Duschnes to Mr. Linton Massey saying that
the story was submitted to Random House for a collection of
stories before Random House was Faulkner's publisher, but that
the volume did not go through because of contractual difficulties with Harrison Smith, Faulkner's publisher at the time.
Either form of publication is possible. Random House specialized
in limited editions at this time; it was not yet a full-fledged
trade publisher. It had a strong interest in Faulkner's work. At
about the same date, Cerf proposed to Faulkner that Random
House publish an edition of *The Sound and the Fury* using
colored ink in the Benjy section to identify the time levels.[42]

It seems obvious, at least, that "Portrait of Elmer" dates
from Faulkner's most creative years and not from his apprenticeship. The quality of the writing, if not of the conception,
bears this out, and the existence of the story seems to confirm
that by this time Faulkner was a serious novelist who wrote
short stories rapidly and skillfully to help earn the money he
needed to finance the writing of more ambitious, more difficult novels, which did not sell. Faulkner's stories were just
like his work in Hollywood, which began shortly after the
writing of *Light in August,* except they were a lot better. It
seems likely that he put "Portrait of Elmer" together out of
his memories—and a possible re-reading—of "Elmer" in order
to make some quick cash, but that he did the job well. Though
comic, "Portrait of Elmer" remains a serious and personal story
in which Faulkner had all his material under control.

"Portrait of Elmer" begins in France with Elmer and Angelo
at the famous Montmartre cafe, the Dome.[43] Near them is

---

[42] See James B. Meriwether, "Notes on the Textual History of *The
Sound and the Fury,*" *PBSA,* 56 (Third Quarter, 1962), 305-06, and
Meriwether, "An Introduction for *The Sound and the Fury,*" *Southern
Review,* 8 n. s. (Autumn 1972), 705-08.

[43] Among the Elmer papers are some manuscript passages entitled
"Dome," "Montparnasse," and "Texas." "Montparnasse," the only one
that is actually descriptive, deserves quotation: "The confluence of
these gray rues Montparnasse and Raspail: the confluence of dreams
and the shaped receptive womb of desire prone, receptive: the dark
woman the dark mother incestuous lying bastioned by gray walls
violet roofed and potted smugly with tile against a paling sky." A

Elmer's portfolio. The flashbacks sketch Elmer's significant past: he thinks of Jo-Addie—"young thin ugly tree" (PoE, p. 10)—and about an old set of watercolors with a particularly dynamic blue.[44] The episode of his infatuation, and disillusionment, with the handsome schoolboy, long and laborious in the unfinished novel, is handled nicely; all that remains from the elaborate piece in "Elmer" is how the boy with "cruel beauty" wrote "finis" to Elmer's adoration by tripping him. Elmer's initiation into the mysteries of heterosexual love is directly related to his becoming an artist: the girl is "unvague concrete and alive: a girl with impregnable virginity to time or circumstance; darkhaired small and proud, casting him bones fiercely as though he were a dog." The encounter leads him to try to paint people and "imbue them with . . . splendor and speed"[45] (PoE, p. 18). His memories of the family's wanderings resemble Joe Christmas's flight down the long street of his past; he recalls "that long series of houses exactly like [one another], stretching behind him like an endless street into that time when he would wake in the dark beside Jo" (PoE, p. 21). Ethel, the bastard child in Houston, the shiftless father and the oil well, Myrtle, the war, an adolescent attachment to a school teacher,[46] the trouble in Venice, the acquisition of Angelo—all these circumstances are sketched quickly. There are echoes of Eliot ("beneath a sky like a patient etherized and dying after an operation" [PoE, p. 25]) and of the symbolists and Impressionists ("Musical with motion Montparnasse and Raspail: evening dissolves swooning: a thin odor of heliotrope become visible: with lights spangling yellow green and red" [PoE, p. 39]). The satire is somewhat sharper. The Freudianism of Elmer's love for the tubes of paint becomes low-comedy vaudeville in a

portion of this description is in both "Elmer" and "Portrait of Elmer." "Dome" begins "Brothers and a sister I had once. I seem to see them shed like leaves. . . ." Both passages are appropriately written in purple ink.

44 A cancelled passage in "Elmer" (TS, p. 33) refers also to his "blue" period.

45 Compare Charlotte Rittenmeyer's desire to use her watercolors to capture the deer she has seen at the Wisconsin lake: "That's what I was trying to make! . . . Not the animals, the dogs and deer and horses: the motion, the speed" (TWP, p. 100).

46 The episode involving the teacher is missing from "Elmer," but may be contained in the ten pages found with the Rowanoak papers.

scene where he goes to buy equipment. He wants the best, and the saleslady does not know what he means. The proprietor understands that he is a rich American and sells him the biggest and most expensive set, "the vun that vill paint the most pictures" (PoE, p. 47). Elmer doesn't know French; he tells the cabbie to take them to the "rive gauche."[47] But when Angelo reveals that Elmer is a "millionair Americain," they are carried to a fancy hotel. Later Elmer moves to Montmartre, settling on the Rue Servandoni, where Faulkner lived, because the landlady is like his mother.

In the cafe scenes we learn that Elmer has painted a picture, a single watercolor. Angelo would like to taste more of the pleasures of Paris, but Elmer has carried him to the country in pursuit of art. Angelo speaks contemptuously of the "seven days of one week . . . we spent in the forest of Meudon while you made a picture of three trees and an inferior piece of an inferior river" (PoE, p. 40). "We might as well be in heaven," Angelo exclaims. "In America even, where there is nothing save money and work" (PoE, p. 40). Elmer intends to stake his career on this watercolor. He is serious about painting. "I want it to be hard. I want it to be cruel, taking something out of me each time. I want never to be completely satisfied with any of [my pictures], so that I shall always paint again" (PoE, p. 51). He plans to present the finished work to a painting master in order to win an apprenticeship. Myrtle is on his mind; her "shortlegged body" and her "lemoncolored dress" become leading images, like the repetition of the refrain "musical with motion Montparnasse." First he will paint, *"and then fame. And then Myrtle"* (PoE, p. 51).

At this moment, as he is reflecting on the difficulties of art and its rewards, he has a visitation of what seems at first the divine afflatus. "It is then that he feels the first lazy, implacable waking of his entrails" (PoE, p. 51). He leaps from

---

[47] The appropriateness of this joke is affirmed by an anecdote from the same period told about a New Orleans artist named Knute Heldner who also took the obligatory trip to Paris in the 1920s, knowing no French and nothing about Paris except that it was the place for a young artist to be. When he and his wife arrived in the city, he told the cabbie simply "Montmartre." Related to me by Dr. M. L. Johnson of Georgia State University, who heard it from Heldner's widow in the 1950's when she bought one of his paintings.

his chair, grabs the portfolio, and heads for his studio apartment, "as though he now carries life, volition, all, cradled dark and sightless in his pelvic girdle" (PoE, p. 54). He is going to the W.C., not to brush and palette, "his life supine before the secret implacable eyeless life of his own entrails like an immolation" (PoE, p. 55).[48] When he gets to the apartment, he discovers that Myrtle and her mother are there. If he doesn't hurry, they will leave without seeing him. The niche that holds the old newspapers for the necessary office is empty. In his necessity, he used the watercolor. The story ends at this point, dying with an ironic closing cadence like the ones Faulkner used to round off *Sartoris* and *Sanctuary:*

> And now the hour, the moment, has come. Within the [Luxembourg] Garden, beyond the dusk and the slow gateward throng, the hidden bugle begins. Out of the secret dusk the grave brazen notes come, overtaking the people, passing the caped policeman at the gates, and about the city dying where beneath the waxing and the bloodless moon evening has found itself. Yet still within the formal twilight of the trees the bugle sounds, measured, arrogant, sad.[49] (PoE, pp. 56-57)

---

[48] In *The Wild Palms,* Charlotte Rittenmeyer suffers a symbolic immolation, too, dying on the dead beach of the effects upon her "entrails" of the botched abortion. She lies in a catafalque-like beach chair while her lover gathers needless firewood. The scene is modeled after Canto XIV of Dante's *Inferno,* in which the poet visits the third ring of the seventh circle, where are punished those who, like Harry and Charlotte, have sinned against Nature and Art. Elmer has "upon his face that rapt, inturned expression of a dyspeptic, as though he is listening to his insides" (PoE, p. 5), while the middle-aged doctor thinks of Charlotte as someone who listens to one of her own "flagging organs" (*TWP*, p. 5). Further carryovers from "Elmer" even seem to include the dark wind that troubles Harry and the doctor in chapters one and nine of *The Wild Palms;* Elmer looks for the missing newspaper in the W. C.: "he looks at the empty niche, surrounded by the derisive whistling of that dark wind as though it were the wind which had blown the niche empty" (PoE, p. 55).

[49] The ending of *Sanctuary* is similar in tone and language: "from beneath her smart new hat she seemed to follow with her eyes the waves of music, to dissolve into the dying brasses, across the pool and the opposite semicircle of trees where at sombre intervals the dead tranquil queens in stained marble mused, and on into the sky lying prone and vanquished in the embrace of the season of rain and death" ([New York: Cape and Smith, 1931], p. 380). Both passages evoke the Luxembourg Gardens. Mr. Linton Massey, the Faulkner collector, has mentioned seeing a letter written from Europe during Faulkner's 1925 trip which included a paragraph of prose very close, Mr. Massey felt, to the present ending of *Sanctuary.* In the letter Faulkner told his mother, to whom it was written, what a fine paragraph it was, and he wondered if he would ever be able to write as fine a passage again. Interview with Mr. Massey, 8 December 1972.

There is danger in overestimating the importance of early and unfinished work like the Elmer papers. Hepburn's view that "Elmer" embodies a deliberate *ars poetica* seems too ambitious, but Oldenburg's statement that in "Elmer" Faulkner tried to write a serious novel about art and the artist is doubtless true. The comedy, so much of it poor, may make one overlook the seriousness underneath. *Mosquitoes,* also generally comic, satirizes the pretensions of certain kinds of artists. Both it and "Elmer" play up the excuses and distractions to which the would-be artist succumbs. Faulkner wrote these satires, we may assume, not because he rated art and artists low, but because he put art at a premium and held the highest standards for the artist. The comedy of "Elmer" and the shaggy scatalogical joke into which it translates with "Portrait of Elmer" are ironic, like Faulkner's preface to the Modern Library *Sanctuary* and his various personal poses—the old eighth-grade man or the simple farmer. No one knew better than Faulkner how difficult it was to create lasting art in a crude, commercial world full of absurd distractions and temptations, nor how often the undertaking seemed futile, nor how little it rewarded those who tried hardest. Measuring Elmer's apparent failure against his dreams, we might remember that V. K. Ratliff, the best man in Faulkner's comic masterpiece *The Hamlet,* falls for one of the oldest confidence tricks in the world, momentarily blinded by a universal human greed. The message of the Elmer papers is that there are not any ideal artists—just as there are no perfect men—in this world. What lies behind the artist is a crazy nexus of fear, love, chance, error, and desire; what lies ahead of him is a constant struggle against his own innate and invented weaknesses. But man's aspirations and his few victories —in life as in art—are thereby sweeter and more necessary to the rest of us.

Faulkner was always capable of self-mockery, even as a young man, a rare trait in men at any time. In "Elmer," as in the interestingly related later novel *The Wild Palms,* he lets foolish and self-deceived characters mouth words that he himself obviously believed quite strongly. Charlotte Rittenmeyer's desire to capture motion was his; the lovers' desire for the best that human beings have ever conceived for one another in terms of human love was also undoubtedly his. And Elmer's dictum about painting, "I want never to be completely satisfied . . . so that I shall always paint again," was, applied to the writing of fiction, his, too. There are passages throughout Faulkner's work which express his attitude toward his art and his talent. In *The Wild Palms,* the tall convict is incensed at the repetitiveness of Circumstance, which has driven him onward using the same old device, the flood: "What he declined to accept was the fact that a power, a force such as that which had been consistent enough to concentrate upon him with deadly undeviation for weeks, should with all the wealth of cosmic violence and disaster to draw from, have been so barren of invention and imagination, so lacking in pride of artistry and craftsmanship, as to repeat itself twice" (*TWP,* p. 264). In *As I Lay Dying,* Darl puts Cash's thoughts about their brother Jewel's nightprowling into the following words: "When something is new and hard and bright, there ought to be something a little better for it than just being safe, since the safe things are just the things that folks have been doing so long they have worn the edges off and there's nothing to the doing of them that leaves a man to say, That was not done before and it cannot be done again" (*AILD,* corrected edition, p. 125).

In Paris in 1925, Faulkner certainly believed that his talent was new and hard and bright. The comic novel he attempted to write, "Elmer," was not one of the "safe things." It was also not up to standard. Faulkner had the good judgment to set it aside and to proceed with new and different work. The effort that went into "Elmer" was not wasted, however; the material and the techniques he had explored helped to teach him more about his craft. Eventually, without repeating himself but without wasting anything either, he was able to employ elements of both in some of the best novels he ever wrote.

KEEN BUTTERWORTH

University of South Carolina

A Census of Manuscripts and Typescripts of William Faulkner's Poetry

THE THING THAT STRIKES one as most significant in studying the manuscripts and typescripts of Faulkner's poetry is the amount of revision and reworking which many of the poems underwent. Evidence shows that *The Marble Faun,* although it may have been written in *"April, May, June, 1919,"* as the published poem indicates, was largely rewritten and its parts rearranged between 1920 and its publication in 1924. Such poems as "The Flowers That Died" and "I Will Not Weep for Youth" underwent a number of minor revisions; there are nine extant typescripts of the first; ten of the second. "Knew I Love Once," a sonnet in its early manuscript and typescript forms and in its first printed form, appeared as a ten-line poem in *A Green Bough* (XXXIII). In short, what we see in these revisions and rewritings is a young artist, studying his trade, learning to use and manipulate words: here is the apprenticeship of the craftsman who would in a few years produce *The Sound and the Fury.* For this reason, a study of Faulkner's poetry is important to understanding the prose stylist of the fiction. This census of materials is intended to aid that study.

Unfortunately, such a study is hampered by the fragmentary nature of many of the documents. In 1942, a fire damaged a number of papers, then in the hands of Faulkner's friend Phil Stone. These papers, now at the University of Texas (with the exception of three sheets which Stone gave to Yale in 1947), constitute by far the majority of typescripts and manuscripts of the poetry. Besides being fragile many of the fragments are difficult to identify or classify since very little of the text remains visible. For many fragments which have no surviving complete form usual methods of classification—by title or first line—cannot be used. In most cases I have used the University of Texas' classification: by first visible line or first complete line. Materials which they have not identified, I have classified by whatever method seemed appropriate: first visible line, line ends, catch words, etc. In such cases I have indicated the method used. All other materials I have identified by title or first line. Where poems have two or more titles I have provided cross-references.

Except for the Rowanoak papers (those materials recently found in Faulkner's home) and several other typescripts and a manuscript in private hands, I have seen all the documents listed here. The Rowanoak papers have not as yet (at the date of writing, May 1973) been delivered to the Alderman Library and made available. I have worked from notes taken on photocopies of these typescripts by Professor James B. Meriwether. Where I have not seen other original documents I have so indicated in the entry.

My thanks are due to Professor James B. Meriwether, who suggested the project and provided me with the information he had collected on the poetry, and to the staffs at the Alderman Library, the Berg Collection of the New York Public Library, the Humanities Research Center in Austin and the Beinecke Library for their courtesy and help. And I am grateful to Mrs. Jill Faulkner Summers for permission to quote briefly from unpublished poems and fragments in order to identify them.

* * * * *

Book Appearances of Faulkner's Poetry

Separate Publications:
The Marble Faun. Boston: The Four Seas Company, 1924.
    The Marble Faun and A Green Bough. New York: Random House, 1965. (Photographic facsimiles of the original texts.)
A Green Bough. New York: Smith and Haas, 1933. (See above for the 1965 reprint.) Two translations of *A Green Bough* have appeared:

    Le rameau vert, tr. R. N. Raimbault. Paris: Gallimard, 1955. Parallel English and French texts.
    Ein grüner Zweig, tr. Hans Hennecke. Zürich: Frets & Wasmuth, 1957. Contains 25 of the 44 poems in the original with parallel English and German texts. (Published in the same year in Stuttgart by Goverts.)

Anthologies:

Anthology of Magazine Verse for 1925 and Yearbook of American Poetry, ed. William Stanley Braithwaite. Boston: B. J. Brimmer Company, 1925. Contains "The Lilacs."

Salmagundi, ed. Paul Romain. Milwaukee: The Casanova Press, 1932. Contains "The Faun," "Dying Gladiator," "Portrait," "The Lilacs," and "L'Apres Midi d'un Faun."

An Anthology of the Younger Poets, ed. Oliver Wells. Philadelphia: The Centaur Press, 1932. Contains "I Will Not Weep for Youth," "My Epitaph," "To a Virgin," "Winter Is Gone," "Knew I Love Once," and "Twilight."

Mississippi Verse, ed. Alice James. Chapel Hill: The University of North Carolina Press, 1934. Contains "Mirror of Youth," "The Courtesan Is Dead," "Green Is the Water," "If There Be Grief," "Here He Stands," "Boy and Eagle," and "Mother and Child."

William Faulkner: Early Prose and Poetry, ed. Carvel Collins. Boston: Little, Brown and Company, 1962. Contains all Faulkner's poems published before *The Marble Faun*. (Textually less significant is *Faulkner's University Pieces*, ed. Carvel Collins. Tokyo: Kenkyusha Limited, 1962, which contains the poems that appeared first in publications of the University of Mississippi.)

The following works I have cited by short-title in my lists:

Faulkner, William. *Mosquitoes*. New York: Boni and Liveright, 1927.

Faulkner, William. *Soldiers' Pay*. New York: Boni and Liveright, 1926.

Faulkner, William. *This Earth*. New York: The Equinox Cooperative Press, 1932.

Massey, Linton R. *"Man Working," 1919-1962: William Faulkner*. Charlottesville: Bibliographical Society of the University of Virginia, 1968.

Meriwether, James B. *The Literary Career of William Faulkner: A Bibliographical Study*. Princeton: Princeton University Library, 1961.

Ole Miss, the Yearbook of the University of Mississippi, Volume XXIV, 1919-1920. [University of Mississippi, 1920].

The Ole Miss, 1920-1921, [the Yearbook of the University of Mississippi] Volume XXV. [University of Mississippi, 1921].

I have used the following system of initials to indicate the location of documents:

NYPL-B—The Berg Collection, New York Public Library.
UT—The Humanities Research Center, University of Texas.

UVa—The Alderman Library, University of Virginia.
YU—The Beinecke Library, Yale University.

Since the poems in *A Green Bough* were printed without titles,
I provide here, to facilitate the use of my list, the titles given
them in other printings, manuscripts and typescripts. Poems
for which titles were never assigned may be found listed by
their first lines.

I	"The Lilacs"
II	"Marriage"
III	"The Cave" and "Floyd Collins"
IV	"Guidebook"
V	"Philosophy"
VI	"Man Comes, Man Goes"
VII	"Night Piece"
X	"Twilight"
XIV	"The Gallows"
XVI	"Puck and Death" and "Mirror of Youth"
XVII	"On Seeing the Winged Victory for the First Time"
XVIII	"A Dead Pilot" and "Boy and Eagle"
XIX	"Drowning"; "Green Is the Water"; and "Overboard A: man"
XX	"Orpheus" and "Here He Stands"
XXI	"Roland"
XXV	"Eros"
XXVI	"Eros After" and "And After"
XXVIII	"Wild Geese" and "Over the World's Rim"
XXIX	"Pregnacy" [sic]
XXX	"November 11"; "Gray the Day"; and "Soldier"
XXXI	"Armistice" and "The Husbandman"
XXXII	"La Lune ne Grade [sic] Aucune Rancune"
XXXIII	"Knew I Love Once"
XXXIV	"Nativity"; "Mother and Child"; and "The Ship of Night"
XXXV	"Indian Summer" and "The Courtesan Is Dead"
XXXVI	"Spring"
XXXVII	"Cleopatra" and "The Race's Splendor"
XXXVIII	"Hermaphroditus"
XXXIX	"To a Virgin"
XL	"She Lies Sleeping"
XLI	"Old Satyr"
XLII	"Sonnet" and "March"
XLIII	"In the Spring a Young Man's Fancy-----"
XLIV	"My Epitaph"; *This Earth;* "If There Be Grief"; and "Mississippi Hills: My Epitaph"

PUBLISHED VERSE

1. a. "A Clymene", *The Mississippian*, April 14, 1920, p. 3.
   b. "A Clymene", Collins, *Early Prose and Poetry*, p. 61.
2. a. "Adolescence", 1 p. manuscript: 28 lines in quatrains, NYPL-B. This manuscript was reproduced in *Phoenix Book Shop Catalog* #100 (Fall 1971), p. 10.
   b. "Adolescence", 1 p. typescript: 28 lines in quatrains, UVa.
   c. "Adolescence", 1 p. typescript: burned fragment, 16 lines visible, 15 complete, UT.
   d. Untitled, 1 p. typescript: burned fragment, parts of 18 lines visible, UT.
   e. Untitled, 1 p. typescript carbon: burned fragment, parts of 17 lines visible, UT.
   f. Untitled, 1 p. typescript: burned fragment, 15 lines complete, UT.
3. a. "After Fifty Years", *The Mississippian*, December 10, 1919, p. 4.
   b. "After Fifty Years", Collins, *Early Prose and Poetry*, p. 53.
4. a. "Alma Mater", *The Mississippian*, May 12, 1920, p. 3.
   b. "Alma Mater", Collins, *Early Prose and Poetry*, p. 64.
"And After", see "Eros After".
5. a. "L'Apres-Midi d'un Faune", *New Republic*, 20 (August 6, 1919), 24.
   b. "L'Apres-Midi d'un Faune", *The Mississippian*, October 29, 1919, p. 4.
   c. "L'Apres-Midi d'un Faune", Collins, *Early Prose and Poetry*, pp. 39-40.
6. a. "April", *Contempo*, 1 (February 1, 1932), 2.
   b. "April", 2 pp. typescript, UVa.
   c. Untitled, 1 p. typescript: burned fragment, 22 lines visible, 18 complete, UT.
   d. Untitled, 1 p. typescript: burned fragment, 11 lines visible, 9 complete, UT.
7. "Armistice", 1 p. typescript: burned fragment, 12 lines visible, 10 complete, UT. This is **XXXI**, *A Green Bough*.[1]
8. a. "Une Ballade des Femmes Perdue, mais ou sont les Nieges d'antan", *The Mississippian*, January 28, 1920, p. 3.
   b. "Une Ballade des Femmes Perdues", Collins, *Early Prose and Poetry*, p. 54.
9. "Bonny earth and bonny sky". This is the first line of XV, *A Green Bough*, which survives only in setting copy, galley proofs and printed text.

---

[1] In typescript setting copy this poem is entitled "The Husbandman." Joseph Blotner, in *Faulkner: A Biography*, p. 1131, states that Faulkner rewrote the poem in 1942, changing one line of the first stanza and adding a third stanza. He entitled it "The Husbandman: November 11, 1942." This version is in Mrs. Jill Faulkner Summers' private archive.

"Boy and Eagle", see "A Dead Pilot."

10. a. "Cathay", *The Mississippian,* November 12, 1919, p. 8.
    b. "Cathay", Collins, *Early Prose and Poetry,* p. 41.
    c. "Cathay", 1 p. typescript, UVa. This typescript is reproduced in Meriwether, fig. 3.
    d. "Cathay", 1 p. typescript carbon: burned fragment, 20 lines visible, 17 complete, UT.

"The Cave", see "Floyd Collins."

11. a. "A Child Looks From His Window", *Contempo,* 2 (May 25, 1932), 3.
    b. "A Child Looks from his Window", 1 p. typescript, UVa.
    c. "If Cats could Fly", 1 p. typescript: burned fragment, 13 lines visible, 10 complete, UT.

12. a. "Clair de Lune", *The Mississippian,* March 3, 1920, p. 6.
    b. "Clair de Lune", Collins, *Early Prose and Poetry,* p. 58.

13. a. ["Cleopatra"], appeared as "The Race's Splendor", *New Republic,* 74 (April 12, 1933), 253.
    b. "Cleopatra", 1 p. typescript, dated in Faulkner's hand "9 December 1924", UVa.

14. a. "Co-education at Ole Miss", *The Mississippian,* May 4, 1921, p. 5.
    b. "Co-education at Ole Miss", Collins, *Early Prose and Poetry,* p. 77.

"The Courtesan Is Dead", see "Indian Summer."

15. a. "A Dead Pilot", 1 p. typescript; at upper left is typed "William Faulkner/Oxford, Miss"; UT. This is XVIII, *A Green Bough.*
    b. "A Dead Pilot", 1 p. typescript; at upper left is typed "William Faulkner/Oxford, Miss"; I have not seen the original; in 1958 it was in the possession of Phil Stone; present location unknown (information from Professor James B. Meriwether).
    c. " . . . ches in Aeroplane", 1 p. typescript; burned fragment, parts of 17 lines and title visible, UT.

16. a. "Drowning", 1 p. typescript, dated "2 April 25", NYPL-B. This version has a second stanza which does not appear in *A Green Bough.* This is XIX, *A Green Bough.*
    b. "Drowning", 1 p. typescript, NYPL-B. An earlier draft of 16.a; the second stanza is defective.
    c. "Drowning", 1 p. typescript: burned fragment, 16 lines visible, 4 complete, UT.
    d. "Drowning", 1 p. typescript: burned fragment, 15 lines visible, 8 complete, UT.

17. a. "Dying Gladiator", *Double Dealer,* 7 (January-February 1925), 85.
    b. "Dying Gladiator", Collins, *Early Prose and Poetry,* p. 113.
    c. Untitled, 1 p. typescript: burned fragment, parts of 11 lines visible, UT.
    d. Untitled, 1 p. typescript: burned fragment, 15 lines visible, 11 lines complete, UT.

18. a. ["Eros"] (This title is given only in typescript setting copy of *A Green Bough*. It is XXV.) Untitled, 1 p. typescript: burned fragment, 16 lines visible, 7 lines complete, UT.

    b. Untitled, 1 p. typescript: burned fragment, 20 lines visible, 4 lines complete, UT.

19. a. "Eros After", 1 p. typescript: burned sheet but poem is complete, UT. This is XXVI, *A Green Bough*.

    b. "And After", 1 p. typescript: burned sheet but the poem is complete except for the initial letter of line one, UT.

20. a. "Fantouches", *The Mississippian*, February 25, 1920, p. 3.

    b. "Fantoches," Collins, *Early Prose and Poetry*, p. 57.

21. a. "The Faun", *Double Dealer*, 7 (April 1925), 148.

    b. "The Faun", *New Orleans Item*, Sunday, August 29, 1954, pp. 1, 18.

    c. "The Faun", Collins, *Early Prose and Poetry*, p. 119.

    d. "The Faun", 1 p. typescript, UVa (Rowanoak Papers).

    e. "The Faun", 1 p. typescript carbon: burned fragment, 14 lines visible, 12 complete, UT.

22. a. "The Flowers That Died", *Contempo*, 3 (June 25, 1933), 1.

    b. Untitled, 1 p. typescript with one holograph revision, UVa.

    c. Untitled, 1 p. typescript: burned fragment, 18 lines visible, 10 complete, UT.

    d. Untitled, 1 p. typescript: burned fragment, parts of 13 lines visible, UT.

    e. Untitled, 1 p. typescript carbon: burned fragment, 16 lines visible, 12 lines complete, UT.

    f. Untitled, 1 p. typescript carbon: burned fragment, parts of 14 lines visible, UT.

    g. Untitled, 1 p. typescript carbon: burned fragment, parts of 14 lines visible, UT.

    h. Untitled, 1 p. typescript carbon: burned fragment, parts of 15 lines visible, UT.

    i. Untitled, 1 p. typescript carbon: burned fragment, parts of 15 lines visible, UT.

    j. Untitled, 1 p. typescript carbon: burned fragment, parts of 14 lines visible, UT.

23. a. "Floyd Collins", 5 pp. typescript, UVa (Rowanoak Papers). This is III, *A Green Bough*.

    b. "The Cave", 4 pp. typescript: I have not seen the original; in 1958 it was in the possession of Phil Stone; present location unknown (information from Professor James B. Meriwether).

    c. Untitled, 1 p. typescript: burned fragment, 17 lines visible, 13 complete, UT.

    d. Untitled, 1 p. typescript: burned fragment, 17 lines visible, 5 complete, UT.

    e. Untitled, 1 p. typescript: burned fragment, 21 lines visible, 7 complete, UT.

f. Untitled, 1 p. typescript: burned fragment, 23 lines visible, 14 complete, UT.

g. Untitled, 1 p. typescript: burned fragment, 22 lines visible, 7 complete, UT.

h. Untitled, 1 p. typescript: burned fragment, parts of 7 lines visible, UT.

24. a. "The Gallows", 1 p. typescript, UT. This is XIV, *A Green Bough*, lines 1-20.

b. "The Gallows", 1 p. typescript: burned fragment, 19 lines visible, 14 complete, UT.

c. "The Gallows", 1 p. typescript: burned fragment, 13 lines visible, 8 complete, UT.

d. " . . . allows", 1 p. typescript: burned fragment, 19 lines visible, 14 complete, UT.

e. Untitled, 1 p. typescript: burned fragment, parts of 4 stanzas visible, UT. (This version has a deleted stanza which does not appear in *A Green Bough*.)

f. "The Gallows", 1 p. typescript carbon: burned fragment, 19 lines visible, 16 complete, UT.

"Gray the Day", see "November 11."

25. a. [*A Green Bough*], 68 pp. [5 blank] typescript with holograph corrections, UT. This is typescript setting copy. In the upper left corner of the first page is written in a hand other than the author's "The Green Bough/Harrison Smith and Robert Haas".

b. [*A Green Bough*], 14 galley proofs with holograph corrections, UT. At the top of each galley is stamped a notation that proof is to be returned by "Jan 27 1933".

"Green Is the Water", see "Drowning."

26. a. "Guidebook", 1 p. typescript: burned fragment, parts of 15 lines visible, UT. At top left is typed " . . . iam Faulkner/Rue Servandoni". This is IV, *A Green Bough*.

b. "guidebook", 1 p. typescript: burned fragment, parts of 20 lines visible, UT. At top left is typed " . . . Faulkner/ . . . Miss."

c. "Guidebook", 1 p. typescript: burned fragment, parts of 13 lines visible, UT.

d. Untitled, 1 p. typescript: burned fragment, 19 lines visible, 13 complete, UT.

e. Untitled, 1 p. typescript: burned fragment, parts of 15 lines visible, UT.

f. Untitled, 1 p. typescript: burned fragment, parts of 18 lines visible, UT.

g. Untitled, 1 p. typescript: burned fragment, parts of 5 lines visible, UT. At bottom left is typed "Paris/27 Aug 1925".

h. Untitled, 1 p. typescript: burned fragment, last 5 lines of poem complete, UT.

i. Untitled, 1 p. typescript: burned fragment, last 4 lines of poem complete, UT.

j. Untitled, *Mosquitoes,* p. 249. Five lines from the poem appear with several differences.

k. Untitled, *Mosquitoes* typescript, ff. 332-333, UVa. The same 5 lines as 26. j appear with minor differences in punctuation.

27. ["He furrows the brown earth, doubly sweet"]. This is the first line of VIII, *A Green Bough.* Untitled, 1 p. typescript, parts of first 3 stanzas visible, 7 lines complete, UT.

28. a. "Hermaphroditus", *Mosquitoes,* p. 252. This is XXXVIII, *A Green Bough.*

b. "Hermaphroditus", *Mosquitoes* typescript, with holograph revisions, UVa.

c. "Hermaphroditus", 1 p. typescript with manuscript note; at the bottom is typed "Eva Wiseman/from 'Satyricon in Starlight'"; I have not seen the original. In 1958 it was in the possession of Phil Stone; present location unknown (information from Professor James B. Meriwether).

d. Untitled, 1 p. typescript; burned fragment, 16 lines visible, 10 complete, UT.

29. ["How canst thou be chaste, when lovely nights"]. This is the first line of XXIV, *A Green Bough,* which survives only in the setting copy, galley proof and printed text.

"The Husbandman", see "Armistice."

30. a. "I Will Not Weep for Youth", *Contempo,* 1 (February 1, 1932), 1.

b. Untitled, 1 p. typescript with holograph revisions, UVa.

c. Untitled, 1 p. typescript: burned fragment, 18 lines visible, 11 complete, UT.

d. Untitled, 1 p. typescript: burned fragment, parts of 15 lines visible, UT.

e. Untitled, 1 p. typescript: burned fragment, parts of 4 lines visible, UT.

f. Untitled, 1 p. typescript carbon: burned fragment, parts of 14 lines visible, UT.

g. Untitled, 1 p. typescript carbon: burned fragment, parts of 15 lines visible, UT.

h. Untitled, 1 p. typescript carbon: burned fragment, parts of 14 lines visible, UT.

i. Untitled, 1 p. typescript carbon: burned fragment, parts of 13 lines visible, UT.

j. Untitled, 1 p. typescript carbon: burned fragment, 18 lines visible, 12 complete, UT.

k. Untitled, 1 p. typescript carbon: burned fragment, 18 lines visible, 11 complete, UT.

31. ["I see your face through the twilight of my mind,"]. This is the first line of XXII, *A Green Bough,* which survives only in the setting copy, galley proof and printed text.

"If Cats Could Fly", see "A Child Looks from his Window."

"If There Be Grief", see "My Epitaph."

32. a. ["In the Spring a Young Man's Fancy-----"]. Untitled, 1 p. typescript, UVa (Rowanoak Papers). This is XLIII, *A Green Bough.*

   b. "In the Spring a Young Man's Fancy-----", 1 p. typescript: burned fragment, 13 lines visible, 9 complete, UT.

   c. Untitled, 1 p. typescript: burned fragment, 14 lines visible, 11 complete, UT.

   d. Untitled, 1 p. typescript: burned fragment, 14 lines visible, 10 complete, UT. Contains holograph corrections; at bottom left is typed "off Minorca/ 1 Aug 1925".

33. a. "Indian Summer", 1 p. typescript: burned fragment, 14 lines visible, 10 complete, UT. At bottom left is written in ink in Faulkner's hand "10 September 1924". This is XXXV. *A Green Bough.*

   b. "Indian Summer", 1 p. typescript carbon: burned, but the poem is complete, UT. This appears to be the carbon of 33.a.

34. a. "Knew I Love Once", *Contempo,* 1 (February 1, 1932), 1. Four lines were dropped from this sonnet when it appeared as XXXIII, *A Green Bough.*

   b. Untitled, 1 p. typescript with several holograph corrections, UVa.

   c. Untitled, 1 p. typescript, NYPL-B. This poem is dated in ink in Faulkner's hand "25 March 25".

   d. Untitled, 1 p. manuscript: 38 lines of trial and revision, NYPL-B. These lines are on the verso of the poem "Nostalgia."

   e. Untitled, 1 p. manuscript: 29 lines of trial and revision, NYPL-B.

35.   "Lay me not the rose for lovers," the first of 4 lines quoted by A. Wigfall Green in "William Faulkner at Home," *Sewanee Review,* 40 (1932), 302. Green states that these lines are from a new collection of poems to be called *The Greening Bough.*

36. a. "The Lilacs", *Double Dealer,* 7 (June 1925), 185-187. This is I, *A Green Bough.*

   b. Untitled [cancelled title: "The Lilacs"], 1 p. typescript, incomplete, UVa (Rowanoak Papers). Added in Faulkner's hand is "Pub. 'Double Dealer,' 1924".

   c. "The Lilacs", 1 p. typescript: burned fragment, UT. This is a separate title page for a draft of the poem.

   d. Untitled, 1 p. typescript: burned fragment, 25 lines visible, 19 complete, UT.

   e. Untitled, 1 p. typescript: burned fragment, 30 lines visible, 18 complete, UT.

   f. Untitled, 1 p. typescript: burned fragment, 25 lines visible, 22 complete, UT.

   g. Untitled, 1 p. typescript: burned fragment, last 11 lines of poem complete, UT.

   h. Untitled, 1 p. typescript carbon: burned fragment, 23 lines visible, 8 complete, UT.

i. Untitled, 1 p. typescript carbon: burned fragment, 23 lines visible, 12 complete, UT.

j. Untitled, 1 p. typescript carbon: burned fragment, 10 lines visible, 3 complete, UT.

k. Untitled, 1 p. typescript carbon: burned fragment, 14 lines visible, 13 complete, UT.

37. "La Lune ne Grade Aucune Rancune", 1 p. typescript; at the bottom is typed an inscription for Sam Gilmore; UVa. This typescript is reproduced in Meriwether, fig. 4. This is XXXII, *A Green Bough.*

38. a. "Man Comes, Man Goes", *New Republic,* 74 (May 3, 1933), 338. This is VI, *A Green Bough.*

b. Untitled, 1 p. typescript, UVa.

c. Untitled, 1 p. typescript carbon: burned fragment, parts of 8 lines visible, UT.

d. Untitled, 1 p. typescript: burned fragment, 8 lines visible, 5 complete, UT.

e. Untitled, 1 p. typescript: burned fragment, parts of 4 lines visible, UT.

f. Untitled, 1 p. typescript carbon: burned fragment, 8 lines visible, 4 complete, UT.

39. a. *The Marble Faun,* 27 pp. typescript carbon, UT. This draft is bound in soft green covers and fastened with two grommets at the top. It has the titles "Prologue", "Spring", "Summer", "Noon", "Autumn", "Winter", and "Epilogue" to mark its major divisions. It also has minor holograph revisions; and three of the sheets are dated "April, 1920." This version was considerably revised and re-arranged for the 1924 publication. One page of this typescript is reproduced in Meriwether, fig. 26.

b. Untitled, 18 pp. typescript: burned fragments, UT. These fragments appear to belong to a single typescript which corresponds closely with pp. 28-49 of the published version. Only a scattering of lines are complete.

c. Untitled, 11 pp. typescript: burned fragments, UT. These fragments appear to be a part of an early draft of *The Marble Faun* corresponding, but not closely, with pp. 11, 12, 21, 22, 23, 24, 27, 29, 31, 34, 35, and 36.

d. Untitled, 1 p. typescript: burned fragment, 28 lines visible, 25 complete, UT. Corresponds with p. 39, *The Marble Faun.*

e. Untitled, 1 p. typescript: burned fragment, 28 lines visible, 23 complete, UT. Corresponds with p. 27, *The Marble Faun.*

f. Untitled, 1 p. typescript: burned fragment, 24 lines visible, 20 complete, UT. Corresponds with p. 26, *The Marble Faun.*

g. Untitled, 1 p. typescript: burned fragment, 20 lines visible, 18 complete, UT. Appears to be an early version of p. 33, *The Marble Faun.*

h. Untitled, 1 p. typescript: burned fragment, parts of 22 lines visible, UT. Appears to be an early version of p. 33, *The Marble Faun*.

i. Untitled, 1 p. typescript: burned fragment, 22 lines visible, 20 complete, UT. Corresponds with p. 34, *The Marble Faun*.

j. Untitled, 1 p. typescript: burned fragment, 20 lines visible, 15 complete, UT. Corresponds with p. 37, *The Marble Faun*.

k. Untitled, 1 p. typescript: burned fragment, 27 lines visible, 26 complete, UT. Appears to be an early version of p. 14, *The Marble Faun*.

l. Untitled, 1 p. typescript: burned fragment, 9 lines visible, 6 complete, UT. Appears to be an early version of p. 15, *The Marble Faun*.

m. Untitled, 1 p. typescript: burned fragment, 28 lines visible, 24 complete, UT. Appears to be an early version of p. 20, *The Marble Faun*.

n. Untitled, 1 p. typescript: burned fragment, 26 lines visible, 23 lines complete, UT. Appears to be an early version of *The Marble Faun* but does not correspond to any passage in the published text.

"March", see "Sonnet."

40. a. "Marriage", 4 pp. typescript with one holograph correction, UVa. This is II, *A Green Bough*.

b. "Marriage", 4 pp. typescript, UVa (Rowanoak Papers).

c. Untitled, 1 p. typescript: burned fragment, 16 lines visible, 12 complete, UT.

d. Untitled, 1 p. typescript: burned fragment, 17 lines visible, 11 complete, UT.

e. Untitled, 1 p. typescript: burned fragment, 13 lines visible, 10 complete, UT.

"Mirror of Youth", see "Puck and Death."

"Mississippi Hills: My Epitaph", see "My Epitaph."

"Mother and Child", see "Nativity."

41. a. "My Epitaph", *Contempo*, 1 (February 1, 1932), 2. This is XLIV, *A Green Bough*.

b. *This Earth*. Contains a slightly different version.

c. "My Epitaph", 1 p. typescript, UVa.

d. "Mississippi Hills: My Epitaph", 1 p. typescript, UVa. This is a 16-line version dated "October 17, 1924". It is reproduced in Massey, *Man Working*, p. 76.

e. "My Epitaph", 1 p. typescript: burned fragment, 13 lines visible, 10 complete, UT. It is dated "16 October 1924".

f. "My Epitaph", 1 p. typescript: burned fragment, 15 lines visible, 11 complete, UT.

g. "My Epitaph", 1 p. typescript carbon: burned fragment, 15 lines visible, 11 complete, UT. This is the carbon of 41.f; together they give a complete draft of the poem.

42. a. "Naiads' Song", *The Mississippian,* February 4, 1920, p. 3.
    b. "Naiads' Song", Collins, *Early Prose and Poetry,* pp. 55-56.
43. a. ["Nativity"] "The Ship of Night," *New Republic,* 74 (April 19, 1933), 272. This is XXXIV, *A Green Bough.*
    b. "Nativity", 1 p. typescript with one holograph correction, UVa.
44. a. "Night Piece", *New Republic,* 74 (April 12, 1933), 253. This is VII, *A Green Bough.*
    b. Untitled, 2 pp. typescript, one pencil correction on second sheet apparently not in Faulkner's hand, UVa.
    c. Untitled, 1 p. typescript: burned fragment, parts of 17 lines visible, UT.
    d. Untitled, 1 p. typescript: burned fragment, parts of last 9 lines visible, UT.
    e. Untitled, 1 p. typescript carbon: burned fragment, parts of 18 lines visible, UT.
    f. Untitled, 1 p. typescript carbon: burned fragment, parts of last 8 lines visible, UT.
    g. Untitled, 1 p. typescript carbon: burned fragment, parts of 16 lines visible, UT.
    h. Untitled, 1 p. typescript carbon: burned fragment, parts of last 7 lines visible, UT.
45. a. "Nocturne", *The Ole Miss, 1920-1921,* XXV, 214-215. This is reproduced in Meriwether, fig. 2.
    b. "Nocturne", Collins, *Early Prose and Poetry,* pp. 82-83.
46. a. ["November 11"] "Gray the Day", *New Republic,* 74 (April 12, 1933), 253. This is XXX, *A Green Bough.*
    b. "Soldier", *Soldiers' Pay,* p. 5. The last stanza of the poem is used as an epigraph for the novel.
    c. "Soldier", *Soldiers' Pay* typescript, UVa. Same as 46.b, except for two differences in accidentals.
    d. "November 11", 1 p. typescript, NYPL-B. The poem is dated in Faulkner's hand "11 November 24".
    e. "November 11", 1 p. typescript: burned fragment, parts of 12 lines visible, UT.
    f. "November 11", 1 p. typescript: burned fragment, 16 lines visible, 7 complete, UT.
    g. "November 11." After this list was in proof, I located a holograph version of the poem in the McKeldin Library at the University of Maryland. It is written in pencil on a Boni and Liveright memorandum sheet. An accompanying letter of authentication states that Faulkner transcribed the poem from memory in the Boni and Liveright offices shortly after the publication of *Soldiers' Pay.*

"O spring O wanton O cruel", (First line of fragment, *Mosquitoes,* p. 249.) See "Guidebook."

47. a. "Old Satyr", 1 p. typescript, UVa (Rowanoak Papers). This is XLI, *A Green Bough.*

b. "Old Satyr", 1 p. typescript: burned fragment, 14 lines visible, 12 complete, UT. The poem is dated in Faulkner's hand "December, 1924".

c. "Old Satyr", 1 p. typescript: burned fragment, parts of 14 lines visible, UT.

48. a. "On Seeing the Winged Victory for the First Time", 1 p. typescript, UVa. This is XVII, *A Green Bough.*

b. Untitled, 1 p. typescript, 7 lines, incomplete, UT.

c. Untitled, 1 p. typescript: burned fragment, 8 lines visible, 7 complete, UT.

d. " . . . the First Time", 1 p. typescript: burned fragment, parts of 7 lines and title visible, UT.

e. Untitled, 1 p. typescript: burned fragment, parts of 8 lines visible, UT.

f. Untitled, 1 p. typescript: burned fragment, parts of 8 lines visible, UT.

g. Untitled, 1 p. typescript carbon: burned fragment, parts of 8 lines visible, UT.

h. " . . . y for the First Time", 1 p. typescript carbon: burned fragment, parts of 7 lines and title visible, UT.

49. "Orpheus", 2 pp. typescript: burned fragments, 43 lines visible, 40 complete, YU. This poem was considerably revised and cut for its appearance in *A Green Bough,* **XX.**

"Over the World's Rim", see "Wild Geese."

"Overboard A: man", see "Drowning."

50. a. "Philosophy", 2 pp. typescript, with one pencil correction apparently not in Faulkner's hand, UVa. This is V, *A Green Bough.*

b. Untitled, 1 p. typescript: burned fragment, 17 lines complete, UT.

c. Untitled, 1 p. typescript: burned fragment, part of 1 line visible, UT.

d. Untitled, 1 p. typescript: burned fragment, parts of 4 lines visible, UT.

e. Untitled, 1 p. typescript: burned fragment, parts of 5 lines visible, UT.

f. Untitled, 1 p. typescript: burned fragment, parts of 14 lines visible, UT.

g. Untitled, 1 p. typescript carbon: burned fragment, 15 lines visible, 1 complete, UT. Has holograph instructions in the right margin.

51. a. "A Poplar", *The Mississippian,* March 17, 1920, p. 7.

b. "A Poplar", Collins, *Early Prose and Poetry,* p. 60.

52. a. "Portrait", *Double Dealer,* 3 (June 1922), 337.

b. "Portrait", Collins, *Early Prose and Poetry,* pp. 99-100.

c. "Portrait", 1 p. typescript: burned fragment, 19 lines visible, 13 complete, UT.

53. a. "Pregnacy", 1 p. typescript: burned fragment, parts of 12 lines visible, UT. This is **XXIX,** *A Green Bough.*

    b. Untitled, 1 p. typescript: burned fragment, 16 lines visible, 3 complete, UT.

54. a. "Puck and Death", 1 p. typescript, UVa. This is XVI, *A Green Bough.*

    b. Untitled, 1 p. typescript, 3 lines, incomplete, UVa (Rowanoak Papers).

    c. "Puck and Death", 1 p. typescript: burned fragment, first 16 lines complete, UT.

    d. Untitled, 1 p. typescript carbon: burned fragment, parts of 16 lines visible, UT.

    e. Untitled, 1 p. typescript carbon: burned fragment, parts of 15 lines visible, UT.

    f. Untitled, 1 p. typescript carbon: burned fragment, parts of 20 lines visible, UT.

"The Race's Splendor", see "Cleopatra."

55. a. "The Raven bleak and Philomel". This is the first line of XXVII, *A Green Bough,* stanzas 4, 1 and 2 of which appeared in *Mosquitoes,* pp. 246-247.

    b. Untitled, *Mosquitoes* typescript, ff. 329-330, UVa. This is the same as the printed version except for several minor differences in accidentals.

    c. Untitled, 1 p. typescript, NYPL-B. At bottom left is typed "1 March 25".

    d. Untitled, 2 pp. typescript carbon; at bottom left is typed "Oxford, Mississippi,/February 26, 1925."; at bottom right "William Faulkner."; I have not seen the original; in 1958 it was in the hands of Phil Stone; present location unknown (information from Professor James B. Meriwether).

    e. Untitled, 1 p. typescript, NYPL-B.

    f. Untitled, 1 p. typescript: burned fragment, 8 lines visible, 4 complete, UT.

    g. Untitled, 1 p. typescript: burned fragment, 16 lines visible, 5 complete, UT.

    h. Untitled, 1 p. typescript: burned fragment, 20 lines visible, 16 complete, UT.

    i. Untitled, 1 p. typescript: burned fragment, 20 lines visible, 10 complete, UT.

    j. Untitled, 1 p. typescript: burned fragment, 8 lines visible, 4 complete, UT. At bottom left is typed "Oxford, Mississippi,/February 26, 1925."

    k. Untitled, 1 p. typescript carbon: burned fragment, UT. Appears to be carbon of 55.j.

56. a. "Roland", 1 p. typescript: burned fragment, 12 lines visible, 7 complete, UT. This is XXI, *A Green Bough.*

    b. Untitled, 1 p. typescript: burned fragment, 10 lines visible, 6 complete, UT.

c. Untitled, 1 p. typescript: burned fragment, 14 lines visible, 10 complete, UT.

d. Untitled, 1 p. typescript: burned fragment, 16 lines visible, 12 complete, UT.

e. Untitled, 1 p. typescript carbon: burned fragment, parts of 16 lines visible, UT.

f. Untitled, 1 p. typescript carbon: burned fragment, 16 lines visible, 1 complete, UT.

g. Untitled, 1 p. typescript carbon: burned fragment, 16 lines visible, 9 lines complete, UT.

57. a. "Sapphics", *The Mississippian*, November 26, 1919, p. 3.

b. "Sapphics", Collins, *Early Prose and Poetry*, pp. 51-52.

58. a. "Shall I recall this tree, when I am old," first line untitled 1 p. typescript; at bottom left is typed "Oxford, Mississippi,/ October 18, 1924."; at bottom right, "William Faulkner."; UVa. This typescript is reproduced in Massey, *Man Working*, p. 77.

b. Untitled, 1 p. typescript, UVa.

c. Untitled, 1 p. typescript carbon: burned, but all 16 lines are complete, UT.

59. "She Lies Sleeping", 1 p. typescript, UVa (Rowanoak Papers). This is XL, *A Green Bough.*

"The Ship of Night", see "Nativity."

"Soldier", see "November 11."

60. ["Somewhere a moon will bloom and find me not,"]. This is the first line of XXIII, *A Green Bough,* which survives only in the setting copy, galley proof and printed text.

61. a. ["Sonnet"]. Untitled, 1 p. typescript, UVa (Rowanoak Papers). This is XLII, *A Green Bough.*

b. "March", 1 p. typescript, NYPL-B. At bottom left is written in ink "15 December 24".

c. "Sonnet", 1 p. typescript: burned fragment, 13 lines visible, 10 complete, UT.

d. Untitled, 1 p. typescript: burned fragment, 16 lines visible, 10 complete, UT.

e. Untitled, 1 p. typescript: burned fragment, parts of 13 lines visible, UT.

62. a. "Spring", *Contempo,* 1 (February 1, 1932), 2. This is XXXVI, *A Green Bough.*

b. "Spring", 1 p. typescript, dated in Faulkner's hand "13 December, 1934", UVa.

63. a. "Streets", *The Mississippian,* March 17, 1920, p. 2.

b. "Streets", Collins, *Early Prose and Poetry*, p. 59.

64. a. "Study", *The Mississippian,* April 21, 1920, p. 4.

b. "Study", Collins, *Early Prose and Poetry*, pp. 62-63.

65. a. "The sun lay long upon the hills," first line untitled 1 p. typescript, UVa. This is IX, *A Green Bough.*

    b. Untitled, 1 p. typescript: burned fragment, 12 lines visible, 9 complete, UT.

This Earth, see "My Epitaph."

66. a. "To a Co-ed", *Ole Miss, Yearbook,* XXIV, 1919-1920, 174.
    b. "To a Co-ed". Collins, *Early Prose and Poetry,* p. 70.

67. a. "To A Virgin", *Contempo,* 1 (February 1, 1932), 2. This is XXXIX, *A Green Bough.*
    b. "To a Virgin", 1 p. typescript, UVa.
    c. " . . . len and Virginity", 1 p. typescript: burned fragment, 14 lines visible, 12 complete, UT. This draft has holograph revisions in ink. At bottom left is typed "At sea, SS West Ivis/10 July, 1925".

68. a. "Twilight", *Contempo,* 1 (February 1, 1932), 1. This is X, *A Green Bough.*
    b. Untitled. ("Twilight" in pencil has been erased.) 1 p. typescript, UVa.
    c. Untitled 1 p. typescript: burned fragment, 16 lines visible, 9 complete, UT. Has holograph revisions in ink.
    d. Untitled, 1 p. typescript: burned fragment, parts of 13 lines visible, UT.
    e. Untitled, 1 p. typescript carbon: burned fragment, parts of 13 lines visible, UT. Appears to be carbon of 68.d.
    f. Untitled, 1 p. typescript carbon: burned fragment, parts of 13 lines visible, UT. Appears to be carbon of 68.d.
    g. Untitled, 1 p. typescript: burned fragment, 17 lines visible, 14 complete, UT.

69. a. "Visions in Spring", *Contempo,* 1 (February 1, 1932), 1.
    b. "Vision in Spring", 3 pp. typescript with two holograph corrections, UVa.
    c. "Vision in Spring", 3 pp. typescript, UT. Has one holograph correction in ink.

70. a. "When evening shadows grew around", first line untitled 1 p. typescript, UVa. The second stanza of this poem was omitted when it appeared as XI, *A Green Bough.*
    b. Untitled, 1 p. typescript, 8 lines, incomplete, UVa (Rowanoak Papers).
    c. Untitled, 1 p. typescript: burned fragment, 16 lines visible, 13 lines complete, UT.
    d. Untitled, 1 p. typescript: burned fragment, 16 lines visible, 9 lines complete, UT.
    e. Untitled, 1 p. typescript carbon: burned fragment, parts of 15 lines visible, UT.
    f. Untitled, 1 p. typescript carbon: burned fragment, parts of 15 lines visible, UT.

71. a. "When I was young and proud and gay", first line untitled 1 p. typescript, UVa. This is XIII, *A Green Bough.*

b. Untitled, 1 p. typescript, 12 lines, incomplete, UVa (Rowanoak Papers).

c. Untitled, 1 p. typescript: burned fragment, 8 lines visible, 4 complete, UT.

d. Untitled, 1 p. typescript: burned fragment, parts of 12 lines visible, UT.

e. Untitled, 1 p. typescript: burned fragment, 12 lines visible, 8 complete, UT.

f. Untitled, 1 p. typescript carbon: burned fragment, parts of 12 lines visible, UT.

g. Untitled, 1 p. typescript: burned fragment, 12 lines visible, 9 complete, UT.

h. Untitled, 1 p. typescript: burned fragment, 12 lines visible, 8 complete, UT.

72. a. ["Wild Geese"] "Over the World's Rim", *New Republic,* 74 (April 12, 1933), 253. This is XXVIII, *A Green Bough.*

b. "Wild Geese", 1 p. typescript: burned fragment, 16 lines visible, 12 complete, UT.

c. Untitled, 1 p. typescript: burned fragment, 13 lines visible, 4 complete, UT.

d. Untitled, 1 p. typescript carbon: burned fragment, complete except for very end of last line, UT.

73. a. "Winter Is Gone", *Contempo,* 1 (February 1, 1932), 2.

b. Untitled, 1 p. typescript, UVa.

c. Untitled, 1 p. typescript: burned but complete, UT.

d. Untitled, 1 p. typescript: burned fragment, parts of 16 lines visible, UT.

e. Untitled, 1 p. typescript carbon: burned fragment, parts of 16 lines visible, UT.

f. Untitled, 1 p. typescript carbon: burned fragment, parts of 16 lines visible, UT.

g. Untitled, 1 p. typescript carbon: burned fragment, parts of 15 lines visible, UT.

h. Untitled, 1 p. typescript carbon: burned fragment, parts of 16 lines visible, UT.

i. Untitled, 1 p. typescript carbon: burned fragment, parts of 15 lines visible, UT.

j. Untitled, 1 p. typescript carbon: burned fragment, parts of 16 lines visible, UT.

74. a. "Who sprang to be his land's defense", first line epigraph to part "2", Chapter I, *Soldiers' Pay,* p. 23. Five additional lines to the verse appear on p. 25.

b. Untitled, *Soldiers' Pay* typescript, f. 25, UVa. The first three lines of this epigraph do not appear in the published text.

c. Untitled, *Soldiers' Pay* typescript, NYPL-B. The first three lines of the epigraph are exactly like those in the UVa Ts. There are minor differences in the other six lines.

    d.   Untitled, *Soldiers' Pay* typescript, NYPL-B. This inserted sheet contains four lines of the epigraph, incomplete.

75. a.   "Young Richard, striding toward town," first line untitled 1 p. typescript, UVa. This is XII, *A Green Bough.*

    b.   Untitled, 1 p. typescript: burned fragment, parts of 6 lines visible, UT.

    c.   Untitled, 1 p. typescript: burned fragment, parts of 16 lines visible, UT.

    d.   Untitled, 1 p. typescript carbon: burned fragment, 16 lines visible, 7 complete, UT.

    e.   Untitled, 1 p. typescript carbon: burned fragment, ends of 6 lines visible, UT.

UNPUBLISHED VERSE

1.   "Above the earth, whose tireless cold", first line untitled 1 p. typescript: burned but its 14 lines in rhyming couplets are complete; one holograph correction; UT.

2.   "Admonishes his heart", 1 p. typescript, sonnet, dated "14 March 1927", UVa (Rowanoak Papers).

3.   "After the Concert", 1 p. typescript: burned fragment, 21 lines visible, 14 complete, UT.

4.   "Ah, spring, that with nightingale rose", first line 1 p. typescript: burned but its 12 lines in quatrains are complete; at bottom is typed "William Faulkner"; UT.

5. a.   "Blue Hills", 1 p. typescript: burned fragment, 16 lines in quatrains visible, 12 complete, UT.

    b.   "Blue Hills", 1 p. typescript: burned fragment, 16 lines visible, 8 complete; has 5 holograph corrections which have been incorporated into 5.a; UT.

6.   "But now I'm dead: no wine is sweet to me," first line 1 p. manuscript: 11 lines, with 9 lines of revised draft below. NYPL-B.

7.   "Cathedral in Rain", 1 p. typescript: burned fragment, sonnet, 13 lines complete, last line defective; at bottom is typed " . . . bove Rouen, in the rain." UT.

8.   "The Dancer", 1 p. typescript: 20 lines in quatrains; beneath the title is typed "to V. de G. F." UVa.

9.   "Dead, O dead, the sorrow loved of spring.", first line untitled 1 p. typescript: 14 lines (not sonnet), NYPL-B.

10.   "Don Manuel", 1 p. typescript: burned fragment, 23 lines visible, 20 complete, YU.

11.   "Elder Watson in Heaven", 2 pp. typescript: 36 lines in quatrains; at bottom is typed "William Faulkner/Oxford, Miss."; original owned by Professor Robert W. Daniel. I have not seen the original but have worked from a photocopy in the files of Professor J. B. Meriwether.

12. a.   "Estelle", 1 p. typescript: burned but the 11-line poem is complete; one holograph correction; UT.

b. Untitled, 1 p. typescript: burned fragment, 11 lines visible, 8 complete, UT.

13. a. "Eunice", 3 pp. typescript: 68 lines in quatrains; several pencil corrections on last page appear not to be in Faulkner's hand; UVa.

    b. Untitled, 3 pp. typescript: burned fragments, parts of 41 lines visible, UT.

    c. Untitled, 3 pp. typescript carbon: burned fragments, parts of 43 lines visible, UT.

    d. Untitled, 2 pp. typescript carbon: burned fragments, parts of 23 lines visible, UT.

    e. Untitled, 1 p. typescript carbon: burned fragment, parts of 11 lines visible, UT.

    f. Untitled, 1 p. typescript carbon: burned fragment, 16 lines visible, 10 complete, UT.

14. "Hallowe'en", 6 pp. typescript: burned fragments, 111 lines visible, 90 complete, UT.

15. "Helen and the Centaur", 1 p. typescript: burned but this sonnet is complete; UT.

16. "Ho . . . one grows weary, posturing and grinning," first line 1 p. typescript: burned, but this appears to be complete; 8 lines; at bottom is typed "William Faulkner"; UT.

17. "I cannot die nor hope to find death such", first line of 1 p. manuscript: 13 lines; below this are 10 more lines but they appear to be the rough draft of another poem; NYPL-B.

18. a. "Interlude", 3 pp. typescript: 49 lines, UT.

    b. "Interlude", 2 pp. typescript: burned fragments, 40 lines visible, 28 complete, UT.

"Leaving Her"[2]

19. a. "The Marionettes", manuscript play of which some of the dialogue is in verse, UT.

    b. "The Marionettes", another copy, UT.

    c. "The Marionettes". A copy which I have not seen was lent by Miss Mary Killgore for the Princeton University exhibition in 1957. Meriwether lists it (p. 9) and reproduces the first page as figure 1.

    d. "The Marionettes". In *Early Prose and Poetry* (p. 18) Carvel Collins refers to a 53-page copy of the play. The two copies which I examined at the University of Texas both have 51 pages; the Killgore copy has 55 pages. Noel Polk in his essay on "The Marionettes" in this volume suggests that the 53-page copy may also be at the University of Texas. See p. 248 and notes.

---

[2] After this list was in proof, I located a 1 p. manuscript poem in the McKeldin Library at the University of Maryland. It is a sonnet entitled "Leaving Her" written in ink in Faulkner's hand. It has one line struck through and appears to be a rough draft.

20.   *Entry cancelled.*

21. a.   "New Orleans", 1 p. typescript: sonnet; last line is scanned in pencil; UT.

  b.   "New Orleans", 1 p. typescript: burned but complete, UT.

22.   "No moon will lighter sleep within these leaves", first line 1 p. typescript; sonnet, UVa (Rowanoak Papers).

23.   "Nostalgia", 1 p. manuscript: rough draft of sonnet, incomplete; 11 lines followed by 6 lines of revision; NYPL-B.

24. a.   "Ode to the Louver", 2 pp. typescript; this poem is part of a letter which Faulkner sent to Phil Stone in the fall of 1925.

  b.   "Ode to the Louver", 2 pp. typescript carbon with holograph corrections and Faulkner's pseudonymous signature "Ernest V. Simms." I have not seen the originals of either of these typescripts of "Ode to the Louver"; in 1958 they were in the possession of Phil Stone; present location unknown (information from Professor James B. Meriwether).

25.   "Pierrot, Sitting Beside The Body of Colombine, suddenly Sees Himself in a Mirror", 3 pp. typescript: 64 lines; at the bottom is typed "William Faulkner,/Oxford, Miss." and below this is written in the author's hand "Written while visiting in the home/Mr & Mrs Ben F. Wasson/in 1921." Original owned by Professor Robert W. Daniel. I have not seen the original but have worked from a photocopy in the files of Professor James B. Meriwether.

26.   "The Poet Goes Blind", 1 p. typescript carbon: burned fragment, 20 lines visible, 14 complete, UT.

27.   "The Poet's Confession is replied to", 1 p. manuscript: 22 lines, incomplete, NYPL-B. The poem is written as dialogue with four speakers.

28. a.   [Prufrock poem] "Let us go alone, then, you and I, while evening grows". This is the first line of a burned fragment which belongs to 29 pp. of typescript (all burned fragments) of a poem written in obvious imitation of Eliot's "Prufrock." On the versos of 23 of these sheets are holograph drafts of parts of the poem. Also on the versos of two of the sheets is an incomplete draft of Faulkner's review of Conrad Aiken's *Turns and Movies,* which appeared in *The Mississippian,* February 16,1921. This would indicate that Faulkner was probably working on the poem in 1920 and 1921. UT.

  b.   Untitled, 1 p. manuscript: burned fragment, parts of 14 lines visible, UT. Although not a part of 28.a, this Ms appears to belong to the "Prufrock" poem.

29.   "The River", 1 p. typescript: burned fragment, 16 lines visible, 12 complete, UT.

30.   "She is like a tower of warm ivory", first line of 1 p. manuscript: 9 lines; at top left is Faulkner's signature; at top right, a drawing of a man; original owned by Professor Carvel Col-

lins. I have not seen the original but have worked from notes in the files of Professor J. B. Meriwether.

31. a. "The Shepherd's Love", 1 p. typescript: 20 lines, UVa.

    b. Untitled, 1 p. typescript: burned fragment, 11 lines complete, UT.

    c. Untitled, 1 p. typescript: burned fragment, 12 lines visible, 6 complete, UT.

    d. Untitled, 1 p. typescript: burned fragment, parts of 14 lines visible, UT.

    e. Untitled, 1 p. typescript carbon: burned fragment, parts of 11 lines visible, UT.

    f. Untitled, 1 p. typescript carbon: burned fragment, 20 lines visible, 16 complete, UT.

32. a. "Sweet will it be to us who sleep", first line untitled 1 p. typescript: 12 lines in quatrains, UVa.

    b. Untitled, 1 p. typescript: burned fragment, 12 lines visible, 11 complete, UT.

    c. Untitled, 1 p. typescript carbon: burned but the poem is complete, UT.

    d. Untitled, 1 p. typescript carbon: burned fragment, parts of 12 lines visible, UT.

    e. Untitled, 1 p. typescript carbon: burned fragment, parts of 12 lines visible, UT.

33.   "Symphony", 4 pp. typescript: burned fragments, 88 lines visible, 71 complete, UT.

34. a. "To Elise:", 1 p. typescript: 16 lines in quatrains; at the top is written in Faulkner's hand *"Dedication";* at bottom is typed "5 December, 1924"; UVa.

    b. Untitled, 1 p. typescript: burned fragment, parts of 6 lines visible, UT.

35.   "To Spring, in Winter", 1 p. typescript: burned fragment; sonnet; 14 lines visible, 12 complete, UT.

36.   "Two Puppets in a Fifth Avenue Wind . . . ", 1 p. typescript: burned fragment, 21 lines visible, 12 complete, UT.

37. a. "Wake Me Not, O April, Now I'm Old", first line 1 p. typescript: burned but complete; sonnet; UT.

    b. Untitled, 1 p. typescript carbon: burned but complete, UT.

38.   "What'll I do today? with twelve", first line untitled 1 p. typescript: 17 lines, last line defective; dated "Paris 27 Aug 1925"; UVa (Rowanoak Papers).

39.   "Wheat", 1 p. manuscript: burned but complete; 15 lines; below these is the subtitle "The Pool" and below it parts of 3 lines are visible; UT.

40.   "When I am gone----and I shall go before you----", first line 1 p. typescript; sonnet; I have not seen the original; in 1958 it was in the possession of Phil Stone; present location unknown

(information from Professor James B. Meriwether).

41. a.   "Where I am dead the clover loved of bees", first line 1 p. typescript: 16 lines; the 2nd stanza has been marked through, however; at the bottom is typed "William Faulkner/New Orleans/10 February 1925"; UVa.

    b.   Untitled, 1 p. typescript: 16 lines in quatrains; dated "New Orleans/9 February 1925"; NYPL-B.

42.   "You and your verse! Do you then believe", first line untitled 1 p. manuscript: 16 lines, NYPL-B.

43. a.   "You are a trembling pool, Love", first complete line 1 p. typescript: burned fragment, 17 complete lines, UT.

    b.   Untitled, 1 p. typescript: burned fragment, parts of 21 lines visible, UT.

44.   "You see here in this leaden tenement", first line 1 p. typescript: sonnet, UT.

UNIDENTIFIED FRAGMENTS

1.   " . . . Aelia, at the casement of despair . . . ", fifth line 1 p. typescript: burned fragment; sonnet; 13 lines visible, 10 complete, UT.

2.   "again/unconquered/hair/in/world"; line ends of 1 p. typescript: burned fragment, parts of 21 lines visible, UT.

3.   "ancient oak/shake/cliff/break"; line ends of 1 p. typescript: burned fragment, parts of 12 lines visible, UT.

4.   "And all the whispering nuns of breathing blent", first complete line 1 p. typescript: burned fragment, 15 lines visible, 12 complete; at bottom is typed "William Faulkner/Oxford, Miss"; under that is written in Faulkner's hand "December 1924"; UT.

5.   " . . . and bound soundlessly . . . ", second visible line 1 p. typescript: burned fragment, 24 lines visible, 8 complete, UT.

6.   "And can the woven fabric's sorry fold", first complete line 1 p. typescript: burned fragment, 12 lines visible, 9 complete, UT. This appears to be a sonnet.

7. a.   "And nymph and satyr follow Pan", first line 1 p. typescript: burned fragment, 24 lines visible, 17 complete, UT.

    b.   Untitled, 1 p. typescript carbon: burned fragment, 17 lines visible, 13 complete, UT.

8. a.   "And your hand strokes the dark", first complete line 1 p. typescript: burned fragment, 16 lines visible, 10 complete; the fragment is dated "July 1920"; UT.

    b.   Untitled, 1 p. typescript: burned fragment, 24 lines visible, 10 complete, UT.

9.   "As tomorrow shall be," first complete line 1 p. typescript: burned fragment, 13 lines visible, 11 complete, UT.

10.   "birth/earth", line ends of 1 p. typescript: burned fragment, parts of 2 lines visible, UT.

11.   "The black bird swung in the white rose tree", first complete

line 1 p. typescript: burned fragment, 17 lines visible, 14 complete, UT.

12. a. "breath/death/experience/brain/again", line ends of 1 p. typescript: burned fragment, parts of 17 lines visible, UT.

    b. Untitled, 1 p. typescript carbon: burned fragment, parts of 17 lines visible; one holograph note in margin; UT.

13. "breeze/tips/lips/leave/grieve", line ends of 1 p. typescript: burned fragment, parts of 16 lines visible; dated "May 1920." UT.

14. "Brief/Of April/What sorrow", beginnings of lines of 1 p. typescript: burned fragment, parts of 4 lines visible, UT.

15. "By this white body shortening into mine", first line 1 p. typescript carbon: burned fragment, 16 lines visible, 10 complete, UT.

16. "Concealed pool where she bathed . . . ", second visible line 1 p. typescript: burned fragment, 20 lines visible, 18 complete, UT.

17. "Could she but drift . . . ", second visible line 1 p. typescript: burned fragment, 13 lines visible, 10 complete, UT.

18. "The dark ascends", first line 1 p. typescript: burned fragment, 22 lines visible, 16 complete, UT.

19. "dies/strange/flies/change/eyes", ends of lines of 1 p. typescript: burned fragment, parts of 30 lines visible, UT.

20. a. "flowers/bloom/hours/ . . . overs/ . . . /covers", line ends of 1 p. typescript: burned fragment, parts of 13 lines visible, UT.

    b. Untitled, 1 p. typescript carbon: burned fragment, parts of 7 lines visible, UT.

21. "For a maid may smile and call you true", first line last stanza 1 p. typescript: burned fragment, 8 lines visible, 4 complete, UT.

22. "Forgotten his pints . . . ", first line 1 p. manuscript: burned fragment, 6 lines complete, UT. This is on verso of 24 below.

23. "The fortune of the race is quickly told", first complete visible line 1 p. typescript: burned fragment, 7 lines visible, 4 complete, UT. This appears to be a sonnet.

24. " . . . glad, how peaceful! and an answering echo within him", first line 1 p. manuscript: burned fragment, 19 lines of which 4 are struck through; UT.

25. "Hearkening the pool . . . allaby", second visible line 1 p. typescript: burned fragment, 28 lines visible, 22 complete, UT.

26. "here/invades/fear/fades/near", line ends of 1 p. typescript: burned fragment, parts of 23 lines visible; dated "May 1920." UT.

27. "Houndslow heath/London mail", parts of lines of 1 p. typescript: burned fragment, parts of 13 lines visible, UT.

28. "Inscribes the answer to its life", first line 1 p. typescript: burned fragment, 12 lines visible, 11 complete, UT.

29. "keep/sleep/not", ends of lines of 1 p. typescript: burned frag-

ment, parts of 3 lines visible, UT.

30. a. "Let lisp of leaves and drowsy birds", first line 1 p. typescript: burned fragment, 24 lines visible, 18 complete, UT.

  b. Untitled, 1 p. typescript carbon: burned fragment, 25 lines visible, 17 complete, UT.

31. "Like your poplar tree, aloof and cool", first complete line 1 p. typescript: burned fragment, 23 lines visible, 20 complete, UT.

32. "Listen . . . while night pales," second visible line 1 p. typescript: burned fragment, parts of 3 lines visible, UT.

33. "Luxuriously until night spills", first complete line 1 p. typescript: burned fragment, 28 lines visible, 26 complete, UT.

34. a. "Mary's brain, with last night's beers", first complete line 1 p. typescript: burned fragment, 19 lines visible, 16 complete, UT.

  b. Untitled, 1 p. typescript carbon: burned fragment, 15 lines visible, 6 complete, UT.

35. "Moon of death, moon of bright despair," first line 1 p. typescript carbon: burned fragment, 20 lines visible, 17 complete, UT.

36. "music/windless . . . mine air/ this fade", words from center of 1 p. typescript: burned fragment, parts of 5 lines visible, UT.

37. "O Pan! who binds with fear both beast and clod", first complete line 1 p. typescript: burned fragment, 12 lines visible, 4 complete, UT.

38. a. "Of starlit stream and frostbound clod", first line 1 p. typescript: burned fragment, 24 lines visible, 16 complete, UT.

  b. Untitled, 1 p. typescript carbon: burned fragment, 24 lines visible, UT. This belongs to an earlier draft of 38.a.

39. " . . . once more rise from hands that yet were dust.", fifth visible line of 1 p. typescript: burned fragment, 21 lines visible, 8 complete, UT.

40. "Panted to crown them with her undreamt snows," first complete line 1 p. typescript: burned fragment, 23 lines visible, 14 complete, UT.

41. a. "Pulse, you timbrels, flare and knock.", first line second stanza, 1 p. typescript: burned fragment, 23 lines visible, 17 complete, UT.

  b. Untitled, 1 p. typescript: burned fragment, 24 lines visible, 22 complete, UT.

  c. Untitled, 1 p. typescript: burned fragment, 24 lines visible, 16 complete, UT.

42. "Queen Sappho, in the starry dusk," third complete line 1 p. typescript: burned fragment, 12 lines visible, 10 complete, UT.

43. "Reft me of brain, begot on me", first complete line 1 p. typescript: burned fragment, 16 lines visible, 11 complete, UT.

44. "A rift of sudden . . . ", third visible line 1 p. typescript: burned fragment, 25 lines visible, 10 complete, UT.

45. "The running see . . . out", first visible line 1 p. typescript:

burned fragment, 24 lines visible, 8 complete, UT.

46. "The same old madness there is", first complete line 1 p. typescript: burned fragment, 7 lines visible, 4 complete, UT.

47. a. " . . . ships and men must rise and pass", second visible line 1 p. typescript: burned fragment, parts of 13 lines visible, UT.

  b. Untitled, 1 p. typescript carbon: burned fragment, parts of 13 lines visible, UT.

48. "The silvery scorn of the guard's far horn," first line 1 p. typescript: burned fragment, 14 lines visible, 12 complete, UT.

49. "sleep/worlds/whirls/stair/flare", line ends of 1 p. typescript: burned fragment, parts of 22 lines visible, UT.

50. "So we walk and dumbly raise our eyes," first line 1 p. typescript: burned fragment, 12 lines complete, UT.

51. a. "sound/around/retreat/feet", line ends of 1 p. typescript: burned fragment, parts of 16 lines visible, UT.

  b. Untitled, 1 p. typescript carbon: burned fragment, parts of 15 lines visible; 2 holograph notes in margin; UT.

52. "strange/eyes/globe/fall", line ends of 1 p. typescript: burned fragment, parts of 6 lines visible, UT.

53. " . . . thought: let's buy us love;" second visible line 1 p. typescript: burned fragment, 12 lines visible, 7 complete, UT.

54. a. " . . . three merry men, and three merry men", first visible line 1 p. typescript: burned fragment, parts of 5 lines visible, UT.

  b. Untitled, 1 p. typescript: burned fragment, parts of 13 lines visible, UT.

55. " . . . towers sank down the rushing west." Second visible line 1 p. typescript: burned fragment, parts of 7 lines visible, UT.

56. "weather/fair/together/year", line ends of 1 p. typescript: burned fragment, parts of 12 lines visible, UT.

57. "Weave for me an evening broken," first visible line 1 p. typescript: burned fragment, 4 lines complete, UT.

58. a. "While each one murmurs: Pray for me." First complete line 1 p. typescript carbon: burned fragment, 23 lines visible, 13 complete, UT.

  b. Untitled, 1 p. typescript carbon: burned fragment, parts of 16 lines visible; 3 holograph arrows in margin; UT.

  c. Untitled, 1 p. typescript: burned fragment, parts of 16 lines visible, UT.

  d. Untitled, 1 p. typescript: burned fragment, 20 lines visible, 13 complete, UT.

  e. Untitled, 1 p. typescript: burned fragment, 22 lines visible, 16 complete, UT.

59. "Who in another world and day", first complete line 1 p. typescript: burned fragment, 20 lines visible, 15 complete, UT.

60. "Your bonds are strong as steel, but soft---", first complete line 1 p. typescript: burned fragment, 9 lines visible, 8 complete in quatrains, UT.

61. " . . . your brows with apple bloom:", first visible line 1 p. typescript: burned fragment, 6 lines visible, 5 complete, UT.

Joseph Blotner's *Faulkner: A Biography*, published early in 1974, some months after the issue of the *Mississippi Quarterly* in which this census first appeared, contains references to and quotations from several new poems, and versions of poems already in my list, which have been unavailable to me. Appended here is a list of these materials arranged according to their location, with cross-references to my list.

The private archive of Mrs. Jill Faulkner Summers:

"The Ace", 10 lines, incomplete. See Blotner, p. 220.
"L'Apres-Midi d'un Faune" (Published Verse, item 5). See Blotner, pp. 245-246.
"The Lilacs", a hand-lettered, bound copy dated January 1, 1920 (Published Verse, item 36).
"Dawn", 8 lines. See Blotner, p. 195.
"Old Ace". See Blotner, p. 1131.
"An Orchid", 5 lines. See Blotner, p. 195.
"A Song", 8 lines. See Blotner, p. 195.
"What'll I do today", first line untitled poem. See Blotner, pp. 453-454.

There is also a bound typed volume of 88 pages entitled *Vision in Spring*, which Faulkner gave to Estelle Franklin in 1921. It has 14 poems: "Vision in Spring" (Published Verse, item 69); "Interlude" (Unpublished Verse, item 18); "The World of Pierrot: A Nocturne"; "After the Concert" (Unpublished Verse, item 3); "Portrait" (Published Verse, item 52); An untitled poem beginning "Let us go, then . . ." (Unpublished Verse, item 28); "A Symphony" (Unpublished Verse, item 33 ?); An untitled poem; "Love Song" (Unpublished Verse, item 28); "The Dancer" (Unpublished Verse, item 8); An untitled poem (Published Verse, item 40); "Orpheus" (Published Verse, item 49); "Philosophy" (Published Verse, item 50); "April" (Published Verse, item 6). See Blotner, pp. 307-312.

Owned by Mrs. Norman M. Thompson:

"Aubade: Provence. Sixth Century", 4 stanzas. See Blotner, p. 185.
"The Bloody Son". See Blotner, p. 185.
"Hymn", 4 stanzas. See Blotner, p. 40 of the notes.
"The Sea-Swallows". See Blotner, p. 185.
A fragment. See Blotner, p. 185.

Blotner states on p. 39 of his notes that Mrs. Thompson has eleven sheets, legal-size bond, of poems, some of which appear in *A Green Bough*. Others are unpublished.

Owned by Mrs. Frederick Van B. Demarest:

Carbon copies of twelve poems autographed by Faulkner and given to Myrtle Ramey in December 1925 (See Blotner, pp. 380-382 and p. 60 of his notes):

"Shall I recall this tree . . .", first line of untitled poem (Published Verse, item 58).
"Moon of death, moon of bright despair", first line of untitled poem (Unidentified Fragments, item 35).
"Indian Summer" (Published Verse, item 33).
"Wild Geese" (Published Verse, item 72).
"[He] furrows the brown earth . . ." , first line of untitled poem (Published Verse, item 27).
"The Poet Goes Blind" (Unpublished Verse, item 26).
"My Epitaph" (Published Verse, item 41).
"March" (Published Verse, item 61).
"The Gallows" (Published Verse, item 24).
"Pregnancy" (Published Verse, item 53).
"November 11th" (Published Verse, item 46).
"To Elise" (Unpublished Verse, item 34).

MICHAEL MILLGATE

University of Toronto

Faulkner on the Literature
of the First World War

WHEN THE BERG Collection of the New York Public Library recently acquired the draft typescript of *Soldiers' Pay* it also obtained a number of other important Faulkner items, among them the fair-copy typescript, complete on one 21.4 x 35.4 cm. sheet, of an hitherto unpublished essay entitled "Literature and War." The self-consciousness of the essay's style is matched by the deliberateness of its physical presentation: the typing is done with some care, the lay-out aspires to elegance (with each paragraph beginning almost center-page), and it seems clear that both the apparent misspelling "sqush" and the omission of final periods from the first and second paragraphs are entirely intentional. Though the essay is undated, it could not have been written earlier than 1924, when R. H. Mottram's *The Spanish Farm* was published, and it presumably dates, like other manuscripts in the Berg group, from late 1924 or the first half of 1925, before Faulkner left New Orleans for Europe early in July. It is certainly to be associated with the thinking about the First World War which produced such poems as "November 11" (subsequently published as poem XXX of *A Green Bough* and present among the Berg papers in a typescript draft dated "11 November 24") and which led eventually to *Soldiers' Pay:* interestingly enough, the paper (watermarked "ENDURANCE BOND") used for "Literature and War" is identical with that used for the first twelve leaves of the draft typescript of *Soldiers' Pay.*

The full text of the essay, printed here with the generous permission of Mrs Jill Faulkner Summers, is given below. My thanks are also due to the Henry W. and Albert A. Berg Collection of the New York Public Library (Astor, Lenox and Tilden Foundations), to its director, Mme. Lola L. Szladits, and to her staff. (Faulkner's period after the title is omitted here.)

LITERATURE AND WAR *

Siegfried Sassoon moves one who has himself slogged up to Arras or its corresponding objective, who has trod duck-boards and heard and felt them sqush and suck in the mud, who has seen the casual dead rotting beneath dissolving Flemish skies, who has smelt that dreadful smell of war—— a combination of uneaten and evacuated food and slept-in mud and soiled and sweatty clothing——, who has spent four whiskey-less days cursing the General Staff. (One does not curse God in war: certainly anyone who can possibly be anywhere else, is there)

And Henri Barbusse moves one who has lain on a dissolving hill-side soaked through and through by rain until the very particles of earth rise floating to the top of the atmosphere, and air and earth are a single medium in which one tries vainly to stand and which it would seem that even gun fire cannot penetrate

And one can be moved by Rupert Brooke if he has done neither of these, if war be to him the Guards division eternally paraded, while the glorious dead can both fill saddles and coffins at the same time, in a region wherein men do not need food nor crave tobacco. And where there is no rain.

But it remains for R. H. Mottram to use the late war to a successful literary end, just as the Civil War needed its Stephen Crane to clear it of Negro Sergeants lying drunk in the guest rooms of the great house, and to cut off its languishing dusky curls.

Business as usual. What a grand slogan! Who has accused the Anglo-Saxon of being forever sentimental over war? Mankind's emotional gamut is like his auricular gamut: there are some things which he cannot feel, as there are sounds he cannot hear. And war, taken as a whole, is one of these things.

William Faulkner

———

The specific literary allusions in the essay are of considerable interest in themselves, since they give some indication of the extent to which, in the middle 1920's, Faulkner was fully aware of the contemporary literature of war. It is of course true that Faulkner could have encountered Rupert Brooke's handful of war poems in any number of anthologies, but if his comments upon them are lacking in strict accuracy (Brooke wrote neither of the Guards nor of the cavalry and himself served in the Royal Naval Division) he does quite neatly undercut the naive idealism which characterises the "1914" sonnet sequence. And certainly the references to Siegfried Sassoon, Henri Barbusse, and R. H. Mottram are more particular and imply a more extensive acquaintance.

The phrase "slogged up to Arras," for instance, derives directly from Sassoon's poem "The General" ("'He's a cheery old card,' grunted Harry to Jack / As they slogged up to Arras with rifle and pack"),[1] while Faulkner's "casual dead rotting beneath dissolving Flemish skies" seems reminiscent of Sassoon's "corpses rotting in front of the front-line trench,—/ And dawn coming, dirty-white, and chill with a hopeless rain" ("Aftermath").[2] "The General" is only the most notable of numerous examples of Sassoon's "cursing the General Staff," and everywhere in his war poetry (e.g., "Prelude: The Troops," "Break of Day," "A Working Party," "Remorse") occur evocations of those horrors of damp, filth, and stench to which Faulkner refers in his opening paragraph. Mud and rain provide, in fact, the central motif for the first three paragraphs of the essay, linking in particular Sassoon and Barbusse (from whom, coincidentally, Sassoon had taken the epigraph for *The War Poems* and for the earlier *Counter-Attack and Other Poems*), and the reasons for Faulkner's insistence become immediately apparent from the early pages of Barbusse's novel *Le Feu*, first published in French in 1916, translated into English as *Under Fire: The Story of a Squad* in 1917:

> The earth! It is a vast and water-logged desert that begins to take shape under the long-drawn desolation of daybreak. . . . With its slime-beds and puddles, the plain might be an endless grey sheet that floats on the sea and has here and there gone under. Though no rain is falling, all is drenched, oozing, washed out and drowned, and even the wan light seems to flow.[3]

Barbusse has many such passages, and they are clearly reflected in Faulkner's essay. *Under Fire* also contains battlefield scenes which may conceivably have provided Faulkner with some of the material for his short story "Crevasse": chapter 20, for

---

[1] Sassoon, *The War Poems* (London: William Heinemann, 1919), p. 50.

[2] Sassoon, pp. 91-92.

[3] Barbusse, *Under Fire: The Story of a Squad,* translated by Fitzwater Wray (London: J. M. Dent, 1917), p. 5.

instance, includes a description of a "Valley of Death" in which the trenches "have a look of earthquake crevasses" and the rotted bodies of Zouaves killed in "the May attack" can still be seen in the very attitudes in which death overtook them.[4]

The mention of Stephen Crane in the fourth paragraph— significant though it is for its indication of a familiarity with Crane which considerably ante-dates Joseph L. Blotner's listing of a 1931 edition of *The Red Badge of Courage*[5]—is rendered somewhat ambiguous by its association with the discussion of R. H. Mottram's *The Spanish Farm*. That this is the novel in question is confirmed by the phrase "business as usual," which appears on page 64 of *The Spanish Farm*, but Faulkner rather curiously gives the impression that the attitude is Mottram's own, specifically "Anglo-Saxon," whereas the book is in fact devoted to the exploration of the character of Madeleine Van- derlynden, a young peasant woman of Flanders, who survives the vicissitudes of the First World War as people of her kind have endured other wars and other disasters in the past. Faulkner seems, however, to have read the novel carefully enough—its allusion to "those young men designated, with the picturesque appropriateness of the French language, as 'aspiring aviators' "[6] is echoed in a *Soldiers' Pay* reference to "that in- explicable beast of the field which the French so beautifully call an aspiring aviator"[7]—and if he somewhat misrepresents its focus he is unquestionably correct in his implication that Mottram deals with the subject of war primarily by avoiding direct confrontation with it—by quite deliberately placing it out- side the range of the central character's, and hence of the reader's, "emotional gamut."

If *The Spanish Farm*, as John Galsworthy acknowledged in his Preface to the first edition, was scarcely a "war book"[8]

---

[4] Barbusse, pp. 268-69; cf. Faulkner, *These 13* (New York: Jonathan Cape & Harrison Smith, 1931), pp. 119-20. See also Barbusse, pp. 149-50, and *These 13*, pp. 116-17.

[5] Blotner, comp., *William Faulkner's Library: A Catalogue* (Char- lottesville: University Press of Virginia, 1964), p. 25.

[6] Mottram, *The Spanish Farm* (London: Chatto & Windus, 1924), p. 135.

[7] Faulkner, *Soldiers' Pay* (New York: Boni & Liveright, 1926), p. 7.

[8] Mottram, p. x.

in the usual sense, Faulkner himself was soon to write—was perhaps already writing—another novel of which much the same comment could have been made. It was natural enough that *Soldiers' Pay,* as Faulkner's first novel, should reflect the current fashion (as documented by "Literature and War" itself) for writing about the war; it was no less natural that Faulkner's own lack of direct war experience should incline him to avoid direct presentation of war scenes and to draw, consciously or unconsciously, upon secondary materials for such evocations of actual combat as he felt to be indispensable. If possible "sources" can be identified for some of the narrative details in *Soldiers' Pay*—a phrase from Barbusse, for instance, and perhaps a mild indebtedness to Sassoon's "The Hero"[9] for the introduction of Mrs. Burney and her "hero" son—that is not surprising for a novel in which technical and stylistic influences can so readily be detected. Indeed, almost all of Faulkner's war novels and stories incorporate renderings of warfare which must depend for at least some of their often highly convincing detail upon his reading of the war novels, stories, poems, and memoirs of others.

What seems remarkable, however, is not the borrowing but the marvellous absorption and transmutation of the borrowed—a process already visible in Faulkner's capacity to capture the very essence of the repetitiously presented experience of *Under Fire* in a single sentence of mannered yet memorable prose. What is still more remarkable is the extraordinary persistence with which the First World War pervades Faulkner's work both as subject-matter and as theme—as a point of reference, a gauge of morale, a phenomenon at once physical and psychical with which his characters must come to terms. The works dealing specifically with the First World War belong for the most part to the early stages of his career: a poem like "The Lilacs," a sketch like "Home," stories like "Victory" and "All the Dead Pilots," novels like *Soldiers' Pay* and *Sartoris.* Yet the same war plays a significant minor role in several later novels and stories, and actually receives its most comprehensive treatment in *A Fable* (another "Story of a Squad"), which is not

---

[9] Sassoon, p. 26.

only a late work but the one which occupied Faulkner for a longer period than anything else he ever wrote.

The precise nature of the First World War's importance for Faulkner is a question which criticism has yet to resolve, but he seems to have recognised it as the one event of his own lifetime commensurate with that Civil War which had been the crucial event in the history of his own region and his own people. It became important for him as an artist, perhaps, not so much for its own sake but rather as a source of those permanent truths, those fables of eternal validity, which he saw as inhering in all human conflict: "Because [as *The Unvanquished* puts it] wars are wars: the same exploding powder when there was powder, the same thrust and parry of iron when there was not—one tale, one telling, the same as the next or the one before."[10] Though Faulkner writes here of combatants and not of civilians, the basic perception is not far removed from the one somewhat stolidly pursued in *The Spanish Farm,* whose very title (since Madeleine's farm dates back to the years of Spanish conquest) invokes that human permanence which is threatened but not in the end destroyed by the violence of particular wars. In terms of such a perspective it becomes easier to understand the way in which Faulkner's early insights into the effect of war upon its survivors, as elaborated in the dance scene of *Soldiers' Pay* and in the statements of the subadar in "Ad Astra," can receive perhaps their richest development in the stories of Tug Nightingale, Bayard Sartoris, and Brother Goodyhay in one of the very last novels, *The Mansion,* and perhaps their crispest formulation within the Civil War context of *The Unvanquished,* with its brief allusion to the "many men who return from wars to live on Government reservations like so many steers, emasculate and empty of all save an identical experience which they cannot forget and dare not, else they would cease to live at that moment, almost interchangeable save for the old habit of answering to a given name."[11]

In "Literature and War," written in the immediate after-

10 Faulkner, *The Unvanquished* (New York: Random House, 1938), p. 107.

11 *The Unvanquished,* p. 263.

math of the First World War and in what might almost be called the pre-history of Faulkner's own career, the tone is uncertain, the basic attitude unclear: the acknowledgment of nightmare merges into the cultivation of a smart cynicism. Much the same uncertainty appears in *Soldiers' Pay*, but in *Sartoris*, with its deliberate juxtaposition of the First World War with the American Civil War, Faulkner began to develop that surer, profounder perspective which enabled him—explicitly in *Sartoris* and *A Fable*, implicitly in *The Unvanquished*, the Snopes trilogy, and perhaps even *Absalom, Absalom!*—to deploy the Civil War, the First World War, and later the Second World War in a kind of shadowy interplay dependent upon simultaneous recognition of both superficial differences and fundamental similarities, of the evanescence of the individual and the permanence of mankind, of the ravelled ironies, tragedies, and even reassurances of time's passage.

JAMES B. MERIWETHER

University of South Carolina

Faulkner and the World War II Monument in Oxford

THE MONUMENT TO Lafayette County's soldiers who died in the Second World War was erected in 1947 on the north side of the courthouse in Oxford. It has not been generally known that Faulkner wrote the inscription on the plaque of the monument, and the story of his association with the project is an interesting one.

Phillip E. Mullen, who was then the assistant editor of the *Oxford Eagle,* made the following announcement in his column, "Moonbeams," in the January 30, 1947 issue of the weekly newspaper:

> Interest in the memorial plaque which the Veterans Club is to erect in the courtyard is widespread, as it should be. Serious and sincere expressions that the names of the negro soldiers who died in this war should be placed on the plaque, have been received from Mrs. H. C. Duke, William Faulkner and Jim Silver. I certainly agree.

Mullen stated in 1957 that Faulkner had come to his office to insist "Of course you'll put the Negro names on there; when they're dead is the only time they are not niggers." And he requested that Mullen permit him to compose the inscription for the plaque.[1]

In his column on February 13, 1947, Mullen provided the following information concerning the monument:

> Seeking a distinctive inscription to be placed on the War Memorial Plaque, the following is being considered:
>
> AFRICA ALASKA ASIA
> EUROPE THE PACIFIC
> Dec. 7, 1941   Aug. 15, 1945
>
> THEY HELD NOT THEIRS,
> BUT ALL MEN'S LIBERTY,
> THIS FAR FROM HOME
> TO THIS LAST SACRIFICE.

---

[1] Phillip E. Mullen to James B. Meriwether, April 27, 1957.

It was written by one William Faulkner who, it is said, is somewhat proficient in the use of words.

This was the first publication of Faulkner's inscription. The second was that on the monument itself (which, since there is only one copy of it, would then seem to be the rarest separate, published edition of any of his work). There was one revision: the second date was changed to "Sept. 2, 1945". (See Frontispiece.)

Although he was given credit for the inscription in the *Eagle* announcement, Faulkner's connection with the monument appears subsequently to have escaped the notice of Faulkner scholars and Oxford citizens alike.[2] The monument itself does not mention his name, of course, and Faulkner himself seems to have made no mention of it, not even to members of his own family. Characteristically, in making, for his native county, this public tribute to their war dead, Faulkner preferred to be anonymous.

JAMES B. MERIWETHER

---

[2] Faulkner's friend Hodding Carter, editor of the *Delta Democrat-Times,* referred in 1957 to Faulkner's "public protest against a decision not to put the names of Negro soldiers killed in World War II on the local monument," but he was unaware that Faulkner was the author of the inscription. Hodding Carter, "Faulkner and His Folk," *Princeton University Library Chronicle,* XVIII (Spring 1957), 98.

PATRICK SAMWAY, S. J.

LeMoyne College

New Material for Faulkner's *Intruder in the Dust*

THOUGH HE METICULOUSLY, and sometimes very thoroughly, revised and rewrote the manuscript and typescript drafts of his major works before sending them off to be published, William Faulkner only occasionally made significant changes in his novels and stories once they finally appeared in print. One such occasion involves his novel *Intruder in the Dust* (New York: Random House, 1948), which he wanted to revise, shortly after its publication, although his changes were never made.

In *Intruder in the Dust,* the lawyer, Gavin Stevens, assists his nephew, Charles (Chick) Mallison, Jr., and Aleck Sander, the son of the Mallison cook, and an elderly spinster, Miss Eunice Habersham, in saving Lucas Beauchamp, a Negro accused of killing a white man, Vinson Gowrie. In the latter part of the novel, Stevens collectively refers to Lucas Beauchamp, now considered innocent of murder, and the other Negroes in the South as "Sambo," a term not used pejoratively in this situation. Stevens believes that the Southerners and the New Englanders are the only homogeneous groups in America, though most of the New England homogeneity has been lost. The Negro, too, has a mode of homogeneity which Stevens praises. Sambo has survived certain historical periods when liberty was surrendered to a demagogue and he may even survive the time when freedom is allowed to exist. In Stevens' view, the South must continue to band together against the federal government which has gradually absorbed the personal liberty of its citizens.

About four months after the publication of *Intruder in the Dust,* Faulkner considered adding new material, expanding Stevens' theory of Negro homogeneity. Among his papers, now at the University of Virginia, Faulkner preserved a letter from Robert Haas at Random House, dated January 10, 1949, informing him of the plans to reissue three of his books, *Go Down, Moses,*

The Hamlet, and *The Wild Palms,* and inquiring about the possibility of changing the story titles in *Go Down, Moses* to numbers in order to express better the unity of the book as a novel. The third paragraph of this letter contains the following: "Are there, by any chance, any other corrections you wo ld [*sic*] like made in any of the three books? I know you'll realize they are plated, but if you want slight changes, just say so and we'll fix."[1] On the reverse side of this letter Faulkner typed:

> Mystic trace of Norman, so that in five bundred [*sic*] years or perhaps even less than that all America can paraphrase the tag line of a book by another Mississippian about 20 years ago, in which a fictitious Canadian said to a fictitious Mississippian in a doemitory [*sic*] room in a not too authentic Harvard: 'I who regard you will have also sprung from the louns [*sic*] of African kings" . . . . .'*

This passage, it is clear, is a draft of part of the additional material which Faulkner was considering adding to the text of *Intruder,* as his subsequent correspondence with Haas reveals.

In a letter[2] to Haas sent from Oxford, Mississippi, on "Wednesday" [January 26, 1949], Faulkner apologized for misplacing Haas's recent correspondence. In this letter Faulkner indicated his concern about the title of *Go Down, Moses* and concluded with a short paragraph about some new material for *Intruder in the Dust:*

> I did not receive the copy of the MOSES jacket. Moses is indeed a novel. I would not eliminate the story or the sectuon [*sic*] titles. Do you think it necessary to number these stories like chapters? Why not reprint exactly, but change the title from GO DOWN, MOSES and other stories, to simply: GO DOWN, MOSES, with whatever change is necessary in the jacket description. We did THE UNVANQUISHED in this manner, without either confusion or anticipation of such; and, for that matter, THE WILD PALMS had two completely unrelated stories in it. Yet nobody thought it should

---

[1] The letter is in Box 27 of the Faulkner papers in the Alderman Library. Permission to quote it was granted by Random House, Inc. The letter is unsigned, but it is unquestionably from Haas. See Michael Millgate, *The Achievement of William Faulkner,* New York: Random House, 1966, pp. 203, 328.

[2] I am grateful to Professor Joseph Blotner for permitting me access to the Faulkner-Haas correspondence.

be titled THE WILD PALMS and another story. Indeed, if you will permit me to say so at this late date, nobody but Random House seemed to labor under the impression that Go DOWN MOSES should be titles [sic] 'and other stories.' I remember the shock (mild) I got when I saw the printed title page. I say reprint it, call it simply GO DOWN MOSES, which was the way I sent it in to you 8 years ago.

No, dont [sic] know of any changes in the three sets of plates. But if we ever reprint INTRUDER, I left something out of it which I would like very much to put in. A single page, or 3 to make the smooth insert, will do it. I remembered it last year only after the book was in press.*

In a letter dated January 31, Haas thanked Faulkner for the inscribed copy of *Intruder in the Dust* which Faulkner was sending from Oxford. Haas agreed to change the title page of *Go Down, Moses* to meet Faulkner's wishes, though Faulkner himself was a bit ambiguous about the title; in the January 26th letter he is not clear whether he wants a comma in the title or not. In his final paragraph, Haas wrote: "As for the omission in INTRUDER, if you'll send me the material you have in mind, we'll try to get it into reprints, should there be any." In early February, Faulkner replied to Haas's letter and sent him the new material, in a two-page letter which is reproduced on the following pages.[3]

---

*Copyright © 1974 by Mrs. Jill Faulkner Summers, Executrix, for the Estate of William Faulkner.

[3] These two pages are in Box 11 of the Faulkner papers. There is also a carbon of the second page.

William Faulkner   INTRUDER IN THE DUST

                                    7 Feb. 1949

Dear Bob:

          Here is the insert for INTRUDER re our
recent correspondence.

          Page 156 as set down through end of the
paragraph, Stevens' speech ending: ' .... hide from
one another behind a loud lipservice to a flag.'

                    (INSERT---NEW MATTER)
          'But what will happen?' he said. 'What will we

do and he do, both of us, all of us. What will become of him

---Sambo?'

          'I just told you,' his uncle said. 'He will

disappear. There are not enough of him to resist, to repel,

to hold intact his integrity even if he wished to remain a

Negro. In time he would have got equity and justice without

even asking for it. But by insisting on social equality, what

he is actually demanding is racial extinction. Three hundred

years ago he didn't exist in America; five hundred years from

now he will have vanished and will be no more. Oh, he will

still exist here now and then as isolate and insulate phenome-

na, incorrigible, tieless, anachronic and paradox; archaeolog-

ical and geological expeditions will stumble on him occasion-

ally by individuals and even intact nests in caves in remote

Tennessee and Carolina mountain fastnesses or Mississippi and

Alabama and Louisiana swamps or, generations ago lost and un-

recorded, in the mapless back areas of Detroit or Los Angeles

tenement districts; travellers passing through the rotundras

of the Croydon or Le Bourget or La Guardia airports or the

supra transfer stations of space ships will gape at him intact

                    156. A.

with banjo and hound and screenless mudchinked cabin and
naked piccanannies playing with empty snuff-bottles in the
dust, even to the washpot in the backyard and his bandana-
turbaned mate bending over it, as the Union Pacific railroad
used to establish tepees of authentically costumed Blackfoot
and Shoshone Indians in the lobby of the Commodore Hotel.
But as a race he will be no more; his blood will exist only
in the dusty files of genealogical societies for the members
of what will then be the Daughters of the Founding Fathers
or the Lost Causes to wrangle and brag over as the Briton
does over his mystic trace of Norman, so that in five hundred
years or perhaps even less than that, all America can paraphrase the tag line of a book a novel of about twenty years
ago by another Mississippian, a mild retiring little man
over yonder at Oxford, in which a fictitious Canadian said
to a fictitious self-lacerated ~~Mississippian~~ Southerner in a dormitory
room in a not too authentic Harvard: "I who regards you
will have also sprung from the loins of African kings".'
        (RESUME; P 156)

              Now they were there and not too long be-
hind the sheriff. For though the car etc etc CONTINUED

                    B.

In this section which Faulkner wanted inserted into the printed text of *Intruder in the Dust,* three points are worth considering: Stevens' elaboration on the fusion of the white and Negro races, the thematic link Faulkner establishes between *Intruder in the Dust* and his 1936 novel, *Absalom, Absalom!,* and the reference to himself as the mild, retiring, little man from Oxford. The "confederation" of the white and Negro races would mean that the Negroes, and presumably the whites too, would disappear as races, though small enclaves of Negroes would exist for tourists and archeologists to see from time to time. Thus Faulkner has raised the issue of racial intermarriage to a national concern and not just a regional one. In *Absalom, Absalom!,* when Miss Rosa Coldfield and Quentin Compson visit Sutpen's house in September 1910, they see Jim Bond, the last of the Sutpen dynasty, who represents the degenerate conclusion of the fusion of the two races. Bond appears almost the opposite of what Stevens envisions when he proclaims "that only from homogeneity comes anything of a people or for a people of durable and lasting value. . ." (*Intruder,* p. 154). Yet the Canadian, Shreve McCannon, thinks that the Jim Bonds of this world will capture the western hemisphere and will eventually be fully assimilated into their environment. In a few thousand years, McCannon fancifully projects that he himself "will also have sprung from the loins of African kings."[4] These two novels contain certain common elements (murder, mystery, miscegenation, youthful narrators) and it would seem that Faulkner, by connecting these two novels with a reference to himself, would like his readers to explore these relationships, a suggestion he rarely gives in his fiction.

[4] *Absalom, Absalom!* (New York: Random House, 1936), p. 278.

EILEEN GREGORY

University of Dallas

Faulkner's Typescripts of *The Town*

AMONG THE MOST INTERESTING of Faulkner's manuscripts and typescripts at the University of Virginia are those relating to *The Town* (1957), the second novel of the Snopes trilogy. In this collection are the printer's setting copy and a separate TS. of 154 pages of *Town* material. Still other pages of *The Town* appear on versos of a complete early TS. draft of *The Mansion,* also in this collection. These versos of the *Mansion* TS., when combined with the rectos of the separate (154 pp.) TS. of *The Town,* comprise a nearly complete early draft of *The Town.*[1] In addition, other versos of the *Mansion* TS., and versos of the 154 pages of the separate *Town* TS., contain fragments and complete drafts of a number of essays, speeches, published and unpublished letters, and of two short fictional works. Altogether, this material is an important—and neglected—source of information about the five-year period of Faulkner's career that followed the completion of *A Fable* in 1954.

This article undertakes to make available, by description and quotation, the most significant data from these TSS. Part I describes the separate *Town* TS. and the early *Mansion* TS. in order to facilitate location of material. It also gives a description and tabular analysis of the early TS. of *The Town.* Part II analyzes the most significant differences between the early *Town* TS. and the final text of the work and reproduces four passages from this TS. that were cancelled from the published

---

[1] Pages of *The Town* on these two TSS. can be fitted together to form several distinct chapters, each having its own consecutive numbering. It is not certain that these chapter units formed part of a complete TS., or even of the same TS. But that an earlier complete, or nearly complete, TS. did exist, or was assembled by the author, is suggested by several *Town* pages, on versos of the *Mansion* TS., which have, in addition to their typed (chapter) numbers, numbers in pencil that could only apply to the entire book—e. g., 170, 275, 434. Though not certain, then, it nevertheless seems quite likely that the fitted pieces of TS are part of the same draft.

book. Part III reproduces the most important of the shorter pieces on the versos of the separate (154 pp.) early *Town* TS. and the early *Mansion* TS.

I

The separate TS. of *The Town* in the University of Virginia Collection (Box 18, Series IA, Item 19d) comprises 154 pages from miscellaneous chapters of the early draft of *The Town*. It has no order in itself, but an order can be imposed upon it by arranging its pages according to their correspondence with pages of the published novel. I have arranged the TS. in this way; and reference to pages of the TS. will be in accordance with their inferred numbers. (These inferred numbers appear in brackets in Table A below.)

The early TS. of *The Mansion*, 597 pages (Box 20, Series IA, Item 20a) consists of eighteen chapters; and the pages are numbered consecutively only within each chapter.[2] In reference to any verso of these TS. pages, therefore, the chapter number is given, followed by the recto page number within it.

The early TS. of *The Town* reconstructed from these two TSS. consists of about 477 pages, of which about 26 pages are missing. Tables A and B below describe this TS. Table A shows where pages of each chapter are found in the TSS. The first column lists Faulkner's chapter numbers in this early TS. The second column lists the pages of the separate *Town* TS. in accordance with their inferred numbers. The third column provides the location in the early *Mansion* TS. of the *Town* pages on its versos. Table B lists those pages inferred to be missing from the early *Town* TS.

TABLE A

An Analysis of the Early Typescript of *The Town*

Chapter	Rectos of *Town* TS. (inferred numbers)	Versos of *Mansion* TS. (chapter and page numbers of rectos are given)
1	[1]—[26]	chap. 12 pp. 32—36, 37—38 chap. 13 p. 1

---

[2] Chapters 1 and 2 are numbered as one chapter, as are chapters 15 and 16.

2	[27]—[37]	chap. 12 p. 36-A
		chap. 16 pp. 33—34
3	[38]—[69]	chap. 10 pp. 13-A, 16—20, 20-A, 20-B, 21, 23
4	[70]—[81]	
5	[82]—[87]	chap. 10 pp. 12, 14—15
6	[88]	chap. 10 pp. 7—8, 8-A, 9—11, 13
7		chap. 9 pp. 1, 1-A, 1-B, 1-C, 1-D, 1-E, 12-A, 13—27, 27-B, 28—29
		chap. 10 pp. 1—6, 6-A
8	[89]—[99]	chap. 8 p. 27-A
		chap. 9 pp. 1-F, 2—12
9	[100]	
10	[101]—[104]	chap. 8 pp. 1, 12—18, 18-A, 19, 19-A, 20—27, 28—32
11		chap. 7 p. 38-A
12	[105]—[108]	chap. 7 p. 40-A
		chap. 8 pp. 1.-A, 2—4, 4-A, 5—11
13	[109]	chap. 7 p. 39-A
14	[110]	chap. 7 pp. 34—38, 39, 40, 41—42
15	[111]—[121]	chap. 7 pp. 2, 8—26, 26-A, 27—33
16	[122]—[135]	chap. 6 pp. 7—10, 20, 24-A, 35—36, 36-A, 37—38, 40—55
		chap. 7 pp. 1, 3—7
17	[136]—[147]	chap. 2 p. 59
		chap. 3 pp. 6, 7-A
		chap. 6 pp. 3-A, 6, 6-A, 10-A, 11—13, 15—19, 36-B, 39
18		chap. 1 pp. 7, 7-A, 9—12
19		chap. 1 pp. 7-B, 13—25
20	[148]	chap. 1 pp. 26—34, 34-A, 35—44
		chap. 2 pp. 45—50, 51—52, 54—58
21	[149]—[150]	chap. 12 pp. 10-B, 13-A, 17—24
22		chap. 12 pp. 15—16
23		chap. 12 pp. 1-2, 4-B, 5-A, 6.-A, 8—9, 9-A, 10, 10-A, 11, 11-A, 13, 14
24	[151]—[154]	chap. 9 p. 27-A
		chap. 10 pp. 22, 24—26
		chap. 11 pp. 1—4
		chap. 12 pp. 3—4, 4-A, 5, 6, 7, 11-B, 12

TABLE B

Pages Inferred to Be Missing from the Early Typescript of *The Town*

Pages Missing	Corresponding Pages in Published Novel
[9]—[10]	36-38
[16]—[17]	43-44
[23]	171-172
[1]	262
[2]—[4]	263-265
[10]—[17]	269-277
[19]	277-278
[22]	280
[28]	284-285
[30]	286
[2]	296-297
[11]	308-309
[11]	320-321
[13]	321-322
[15]	323-324

II

SIGNIFICANT DIFFERENCES BETWEEN THE EARLY *TOWN* TYPESCRIPT AND THE PUBLISHED NOVEL

A majority of the chapters in the reconstructed early TS. of *The Town* follow the published novel rather closely. There are, inevitably, a great number of relatively minor variations between the two versions—changes, additions, deletions of words, phrases, and even sentences. They are not insignificant and should someday be considered in a more detailed study of the text of the novel.

These differences are not, however, examined here. This description concerns only those instances of substantial alteration from this early version to the final one. There are three important additions of material: the action of Manfred de Spain as mayor, the romance of Wallstreet Snopes and Miss Vaiden Wyott, and the background of Uncle Willy. Besides these changes, the major revision seems to have concerned Charles Mallison (in chapters 1, 3, and 7) and Gavin Stevens (in chapters 5, 20, and 24).

In the material reproduced below, authorial revisions have

been incorporated into the transcription and paragraph indention has been standardized. Obvious typing errors have been emended; but the original readings are given in the note preceding each passage.

A. Additions of Material

1. MANFRED DE SPAIN: Material in the published novel (p. 13.7—p. 13.36) [3] not present in the TS.

This addition concerning De Spain's handling of Old Bayard Sartoris' edict against automobiles, besides elaborating the character of the "new age" which enters Jefferson with De Spain's election, comments on De Spain's habitual scorn for some civic laws and restraints.

2. WALLSTREET PANIC SNOPES AND MISS VAIDEN WYOTT: Material in the published novel (p. 144.15—p. 146.8) not present in the TS.

This addition drastically alters Wallstreet Panic's story and presents a love relationship which has significant parallels with that of Gavin Stevens and Linda Snopes.

In the earlier TS. Wallstreet's history is the same; he finally, after great effort, becomes owner of the store in which he had been a clerk, and then he marries the young country girl whose ambition matches his own. As the story was originally conceived, Wallstreet saves himself from Snopeses, or rises above Snopeses, almost solely through his own will and industry. But in the final version Miss Wyott, as his guide and mentor, is crucially important in helping to extricate him from the kind of existence which was his birthright as a Snopes. In both versions Miss Wyott suggests that Wallstreet Panic change his name, with all its connotations of dishonest, hollow usury, to Wall, the name carried by a brave Mississippi general. Her role is not extended much further than this in the earlier TS. But in the novel she is a woman who understands Snopeses and the necessity for Wallstreet to escape or redeem his name; so she intercedes in leading him to the girl who, like him, is courageously opposed to Snopeses.

---

[3] In describing, here and elsewhere, material added in the published version, line references indicate only that the addition begins or ends *within* the given line.

A more curious aspect of this addition is Wallstreet Panic's love for Miss Wyott and his proposal of marriage to her. Wallstreet loves "Miss Vaiden," ten years his senior, as a pupil loves the teacher who has taught him with devotion and who is an ideal of constancy for him. Miss Wyott has understood Wallstreet's worth and has attempted to guide him for seven years. But she is shocked at his proposal, because of the vast differences in their ages and stations, and knows that this relationship could not be fulfilled in marriage; so she gently refuses him and leads him to the proper girl, the one intended for him.

It is significant that this addition to Snopeslore occurs in the chapter in which Gavin Stevens describes his first real vision of Linda Snopes. The story allows us insight into his attempt to "save" Linda by being her mentor and guide, not (in the ordinary sense) her lover or husband.

3.   UNCLE WILLY: Material in the published novel (p. 154.32—p. 155.18) not in the TS.

The character in the early version is named Old Doc, but he seems to represent the same character as Uncle Willy. Old Doc's fondness for morphine and Walter Christian's for alcohol are mentioned in the early version, but in this addition Faulkner more fully recovers the characters from the short story, "Uncle Willy."

B.   Charles Mallison: Changes in Narration

Chapters 1, 3, and 7 underwent considerable alteration during the composition of the early draft. The changes involved not the incidents or the stories narrated, but the focus of narration itself.

A more detailed bibliographical study of the pages of these chapters would be necessary to determine more closely, if possible, the sequence of the changes which took place. The following brief analysis, however, accounts for most of the alterations in the typescript that pertain to narration.

Faulkner appears to have originally written chapter 1 and most of chapter 3 with Charles as first-person narrator, directly participating—without intercession by Gowan—in the events surrounding the brass-stealing in chapter 1 and the Cotillion

Ball in chapter 3. But toward the end of chapter 3, on p. 34, he conceived of presenting the story through the eyes of Gowan. About half of this page is typed with Charles's first-person point of view; but in the middle of a paragraph Faulkner begins typing in third-person point of view, with Charles narrating the story *as experienced by* Gowan. The first half of the page shows ink corrections altering the original point of view of Charles to that of Gowan. The rest of chapter 3 is typed in this altered point of view.

Faulkner returned to chapter 1 and the part of chapter 3 already written. He wrote a new beginning for each chapter in order to introduce Gowan and define his position: the original p. 1 of each chapter became 1.-A (recto of *Town* TS. p. [2]) and 1.-A (recto of *Town* TS. p. [39]). He then in ink corrected the point of view throughout these two chapters up to p. 34.

The shift of viewpoint from Charles to Gowan necessitated other changes in chapters 1 and 3. Charles's age is altered drastically. In the first chapter of the unaltered version, Charles says he was "not even twelve then" (verso of *Mansion* TS.: chap. 12, p. 36). In the added beginning of this chapter, however, when Gowan is introduced, Charles says he "was only one or two then, just barely born" (recto of *Town* TS. p. [1]). And in the added beginning of chapter 3, Charles "was still eating in the kitchen with Aleck Sander yet" (recto of *Town* TS. p. [38]). Charles, then, after the introduction of Gowan, is about two years old. Gowan is thirteen, near the age of Charles in the original unaltered version. These changes of age are consistently made along with the changes in point of view.

The early draft of chapter 7 also shows Charles Mallison as narrator. It is told in first person; Gowan is not present. Charles is Ratliff's ice-cream partner, giving him news from Stevens, helping him "tote the load," listening to Snopeslore. The draft of this chapter shows no alterations in point of view: the story is told as Charles sees and hears it; Gowan remains absent. Faulkner in this chapter was evidently working from the revised age of Charles in chapters 1 and 3. It is logical at this point that Charles see and narrate directly, that Gowan be omitted as intercessor. Charles is now old enough to understand for himself: if he were about two at the time of the brass-stealing he would be about six when his uncle leaves for World War I as YMCA secretary, old enough to listen to and learn from Ratliff for two years while his uncle is in Europe. In this early version Stevens does not leave Jefferson again to rehabilitate Europe after returning from service in the YMCA.

A comparison of the early draft of chapters 1, 3, and 7 with the published text reveals that even further alteration has been made. In the final version of chapter 7 Gowan is present again and serves as a proxy observer for Charles in at least part of the chapter. Related to Gowan's presence are several other alterations of the earlier version:

1. Charles's age is moved back about three more years; this change makes him ineligible as narrator in chapter 7 and justifies Gowan's presence there. Consistent changes in Charles's age have been made throughout the three chapters. In the novel he is born while his uncle is in Germany (*The Town*, p. 54); in the original version he would have been about three or four at this time.

2. Gavin Stevens is given an additional two years in Europe after his YMCA service; this change allows Charles in his turn to become Ratliff's talking partner, to be actively educated in Snopeses and involved in "toting the load."

3. A great deal of material has been added in the final version to account for Gowan's presence, Charles's coming-of-age, and Stevens' second trip abroad to rehabilitate Europe. The most significant of the additions appear in the published novel on the following pages: 105.24—106.3; 106.15-29; 107.26-27; 111.4—112.13; 112.30—113.12; 114.23-25; 114.28-29; 116.3-8; 120.10-13.

Faulkner, then, on two separate occasions—once in writing chapter 3 and later in rewriting the draft of the novel—decided to introduce an intervening narrator into what was a direct narrative by Charles. In both cases Faulkner's introducing Gowan might have been a result of altering Charles's age—ten years at first, then three years more—to fit a changing chronological scheme for *The Town* and perhaps also *The Mansion*.

But Gowan's presence accomplishes much more than this. As a character he does not differ much from Charles: that his name was simply substituted for that of Charles in the early draft indicates their similarity. Gowan seems to function primarily as another imaginative filter in the rich transmission to Charles of stories and attitudes from Ratliff, Gavin, and the town itself. Charles's narration through the eyes of Gowan, at second and third remove from the sources, emphasizes the legendary aspect of the events in which his immediate family and acquaintances are involved.

In changing Charles's age and introducing Gowan, Faulkner also emphasizes that the novel is in part about Charles's education. By the time he is actually introduced to Ratliff at the age of five, he has already inherited Gowan's experience and has been prepared to assume an increasingly significant role, along with Ratliff and his Uncle Gavin, in studying and trying to understand the Snopeses. Like Ratliff and Stevens he represents the "we" which is Jefferson. The indirection of his education in Snopeses makes him better representative of the anonymous viewpoint of Jefferson than if he were recounting the events at first hand.

C. Gavin Stevens

A comparison of the reconstructed TS. of *The Town* to the published version shows that Faulkner made important alterations in chapter 5, 20 and 24, all of which pertain to Gavin Stevens.

1. CHAPTER 5. This chapter, narrated by Stevens, has been considerably revised and expanded in the final version. The original chapter has been rewritten completely, with changes in words and phrases and reworking of sentences throughout. But much material has been added. The most significant of the additions occur in the published novel on the following pages and within the given lines: 88.23-27; 88.29—89.2; 90.9-11; 90.33—91.16; 92.1-3; 92.5-9; 92.15-23; 92.26—93.16; 93.19-21; 93.35—94.2; 95.10-11; 95.20-21.

With all this expansion of the original material, the two versions seem essentially the same in their portrayal of Stevens. The original version consists almost wholly of Stevens' musings and his cryptic conversation with Eula. The treatment of the scene is much more concrete in the published version. We are reminded in the published novel that it is January and that a "cold invisible cloud" enters Stevens' room whenever he opens the door for Eula. Eula, too, in the final version has a much more physical presence than in the earlier version.

Besides these changes there is a greater emphasis in the final version on Stevens' somewhat self-mocking view of himself as a defender of Eula's honor (pp. 88.23-27, 90.9-11, 91.10-12). In general he possesses in the final version an even more heightened self-awareness of his position: the anguished fearful lover and at the same time the scrupulous gentleman.

2.   CHAPTER 20. On pages of this chapter in the early draft are several passages not appearing in the published novel. Other pages (on versos of the *Mansion* TS.), evidently deleted from the author's final TS., show these same passages cancelled in red pencil.

This deleted material is here reproduced in full.

A passage in the book version (p. 334.36—p. 335.15) does not appear in the early *Town* TS.

a.   The text of this passage follows that of pages, numbered "1.-A," "2," and "2-A," on versos of the *Mansion* TS.: chap. 1, pp. 27-29. The cancelled passage would occur in *The Town*, following p. 313.7. The first part of the paragraph, greatly abbreviated in the novel, is also printed here in its earlier form. The following typing errors have been emended:

1. 7 thedamned] the damned	1. 19 get at] get
1. 8 threeof] three of	1. 29 and come] come

> The note said ten oclock. That was all: *Please meet me at your office at ten tonight.* Not *if convenient,* let alone *when could you see me at your office?* but simply *at ten tonight please.* You see. Because in the first place. Why me? *Me?* I almost telephoned; a note in return would be too cold; besides it would take too long. No: damned too long: too cold, too gutless: to go in person, into the damned hall, the damned living room and say to all of them, all three of them——no, all four, taking De Spain with me——the damned old ruthless brigand of a usurer who didn't even bother to hide it where at least the town-translated one behind that bow tie took a little pains for circumspection even if it did merely snap, clip together in the back like the tie did;——to say to them all as well as the terrible the terrifying woman who just by having to walk and breathe had caused it all; oh yes, to her, let listen who would: *Why cant you let me alone? What more can you want of me, let alone expect since you probably knew from the first*

what little I had would not be worth your picking up: merely to
worry, to nag and badger and harass like a stingless mosquito until
your aim was finally served and your child did get away to
school, even though it is only fifty miles to Oxford since it is at
least that much security for you because after all children even
of only going on nineteen do begin to notice. What more can you
possibly want of me what is left?

Or simply not to go at all. Yes——because better still——to
lurk in a dark doorway and even watch her climb the stairs and
knock (no: I had unlocked it; I would have to go back first and
lock it again) at the office door, still standing there trying to stand
in shadow and not knock loud yet still loud enough, still trying to
decide .whether to leave before someone saw and come back
later still without being seen, while Otis Harker with his new night
marshal's badge and the borrowed pistol which he had probably
never fired, stalked and caught her red-handed:

'Evenin, Miz Snopes. Kin I hep you any?'

So I would have to go back and lock the door again first. But
there would be plenty of time

b.   The text of this passage follows that of a page, numbered
"9," on the verso of the *Mansion* TS.: chap. 1, p. 34-A. The
passage would occur in *The Town*, following p. 319.19. Parts
of this paragraph, greatly revised in the published novel, are
also printed here in an earlier version.

The following typing error has been emended:
1. 20 thelatch] the latch

of buffoon's folklore.

And now he—Harker—was even instrument of my own fate
and doom since even if I locked the door (there was still time:
ten minutes) and went home, when he finally stalked and, as he
puts it, 'rounded up' on her knocking at the door, he himself would
tell her how it had been no cold inflexible decision but I had simply
at the last moment lost my nerve. Though there were still ten
minutes, and it would take him at least twenty-five to 'round up'
the gin and compress and their purlieus and get back to the
Square. And now I had changed my mind so many times about
locking and unlocking the office door that I couldn't remember
myself which it was, stopping half way up the stairs and beginning
to turn back since the office key was still on the ring with the
switch key in the car (we didn't have to remove switch keys and
lock house doors in Jefferson yet; we were not that civilised yet);
and I know now that even then I already smelled the tobacco
smoke, deciding at last that I had unlocked the door and had not
returned to relock it, and went on and turned the knob or tried
to and then tried again since indubitably I was losing part of what

I called my mind; then the latch clicked back from inside and
the door opened and now I did smell the smoke, she standing
there against the dark [interior]

c. The text of this passage follows that of pages, numbered
"26" and "28," on versos of the *Mansion* TS.: chap. 1, pp. 57-58,
and of a page, numbered "27," on the recto of *Town* TS. p. [148].
The passage would occur in *The Town,* following p. 334.21.
The following typing error has been emended:
1. 4 feel] fell

which is its grief. While I was in Cambridge, obviously knowing
as much about women as I do now since I have it on good authority
——two good authorities in fact——that I know nothing about them
at all, naturally I fell in love. A local girl with a future; she
clerked in a ten-cent store in Boston. Naturally I wanted to marry
her, particularly since I had a rival who really took matrimony
seriously too, I a freshman and he a graduating medical student.
She chose him. But with pity. Oh yes, he had (or rather, as I
thought then, to have) the body but I had the pity. The tenderness.
We had one last date together. It was formal, a ritual, an immolation; you know: one last chance; here I am, inviolate yet,
win me if you can since the field for this last yet-uncommitted
moment, is yours.
  She arranged all herself; my rival himself understood; this
out of both their pities for me; the wedding to be Sunday, this
Friday night mine, the Saturday between her maiden's meditant
to make the final irrevocable decision. I failed of course, which is
purely incidental; we all expected that but were simply gentle
with it; and took her home——or started to. 'Not home,' she said.
'I'm staying with a girl-friend tonight at Number (we will call
it) Blank Brattle street.' And took her there, once more to say
Goodnight and lose dimension and then substance too within the
shadow of the stoop; again I heard a door. Though the rest was by
one of those fortuitous outrages which (as they say) to a dog
should not happen. I forget now even what, perhaps my rival
himself overheard or perhaps even speaking innocently to me: 'No,
we dont live there now. I moved the week before our wedding, to
Number Blank Brattle street.' A dimension less, then a substance
less

These three passages which Faulkner chose to delete
emphasize, perhaps too explicitly, attitudes which are evident
in the rest of the chapter. Passages "a" and "b," describing
Stevens' indecision about meeting Eula, show his bewilderment
at Flem's exposure of Eula and De Spain's adultery, and his fear

of facing Eula, "the terrible the terrifying woman who just by having to walk and breathe had caused it all" (p. "1-A," verso of *Mansion* TS.: chap. 1, p. 27). Passage "c," describing an earlier relationship in which Stevens had been second best to another man, emphasizes the sense of failure and of terrible loss which he feels in saying goodbye to Eula for the last irrevocable time. In the final version, not only has passage "c" been deleted, but a long passage near the end of the chapter (p. 334.36—p. 335.15) has been added.

Stevens is fearful of meeting Eula because he does not want the anguish of being further involved with her. Because to be a part of *Motion,* which *is* Eula and all that involves her, is difficult and painful. But nevertheless he does meet Eula and does become further involved. She tells him what Flem's motives are and have been, and does not allow him the protection of his idealistic explanations. But further than this she makes him swear to marry Linda if it becomes necessary. The passage on p. 335 added in the final version expresses the anguish which Stevens feels not only at losing Eula but also at having become even more inextricably bound to her in assuming the guardianship of Linda.

3. CHAPTER 24. A passage from a page of this chapter in the early draft does not appear in the published novel. Another page (on a verso of the *Mansion* TS.), evidently deleted from the author's final TS., shows this same passage cancelled in red pencil. The text here follows the rejected page of the author's final TS., on the verso of the *Mansion* TS.: chap. 12, p. 31. The passage would occur in *The Town,* following p. 356.31.

until they were all the color of mud and dirt too.

So the thing to do was to have a ball that not only didn't move, it couldn't move: nailed say to a post in the middle of the field where everybody would always know exactly where to look for it and expect to find it, and the aim of the defense was to keep the offense from breaking through and touching it, which would count one score. Or better than that: not just one ball but eleven, everybody to have a ball, each one a different color of course; and the quarterback's signal wouldn't mean where the ball was going because that wouldn't matter because all eleven of the balls would be going in different directions anyhow, and a smart defensive quarterback's job would be to outguess and figure just which color ball would count on this play and get his men to concentrate on that one and smother it. And no boundaries at all, so that a smart fast player could slip out say and lie low and then skirt around and then come in from behind, across town from the opposite direction; going on like that

This passage, related by Charles Mallison, is originally part of Stevens' monologue while he is riding back to his office with Ratliff and Charles after seeing Eula's new tombstone and sending Linda to New York. Certainly Stevens' distracted discussion of football seems odd at this point, and Faulkner may have decided not to prolong it. But the author evidently associated this additional material about football with the episode: though not appearing in the published version of *The Town,* the passage is recalled in substantial detail in *The Mansion* (p. 149) as Ratliff retells the incident.

The passage, reflecting Stevens' bewilderment and grief over Eula's death, defines a major theme of the novel. The football game is here an analogy for Motion, the essential on-going of truth, the immersion in life. Stevens, in a state of distraction at this point, says that the thing wrong with the football game as it is normally played is that everything—the players, the ball, the dirt and mud—are so intermingled that no one can tell what is happening. He contemplates some variations of the game which would avoid the perplexing, confusing motion; analogously he wonders about some possible ways of coping with Motion besides submitting to it. But the comic absurdity of the proposals indicates their worth.

One could stop Motion, pin truth down to certainty: nail the ball to a post in the center of the field so that everybody would know exactly where to find it and could come up to touch it when he wanted to. Or, one could make everything Motion, flux, do away with certain truth: give everyone his own ball and let him run with it, get rid of boundaries. Stevens, involved in the Motion of Eula's life and of her death, now faces the painful complexity of human passion and the frailty of his own understanding of it. The comic analogy of this passage shows that, though he might wish at this point that there were a way to avoid the pain and confusion of Motion, he knows that even to try to avoid it is false and absurd.

III

FAULKNER MATERIAL ON VERSOS OF TYPESCRIPTS OF *THE TOWN* AND *THE MANSION*

The most significant short pieces—letters and other material—which appear on versos of the TSS. of *The Town* and of *The Mansion* are reproduced below. In the letters, published and unpublished, the paragraph indention has been standardized; minor authorial revisions have been incorporated into the transcription. Obvious typing errors have been emended; but the original readings are recorded in the headnotes.

1.

Unidentified note, manuscript; cf. *A Fable* (New York, 1954), p. 199. Verso of *Town* TS. p. [126].

> it was like dream: succint, inconsequential, and bizarre: 'So you came to France to bring him the money,' the runner said.
> Splendid news. stop not that quote the old man ungrate needs more accolade than it already has from us who know the anguish it took and have tried to do it too. Bill Faulkner

2.

Sketch of a genealogy of the Snopes family, manuscript. Verso of *Town* TS. p. [57]. (See following page for illustration.)

3.

Unpublished letter to Mr. Green. See Faulkner's letter to the *New York Times* (published March 25, 1955) in *Essays, Speeches & Public Letters,* ed. James B. Meriwether (New York, 1966), pp. 217-218. Verso of *Town* TS. p. [54].

Oxford, Miss.
4 April, 1955

Dear Mr Green:

Yours of 25th. at hand. I had already seen the NY TIMES letter.

Herewith my qualifications——such as they are.

I have never been a Greek Orthodox Metropolitan.

When a young man I was closely enough associated with communists to learn quickly that I didn't like it, it is dangerous, and that it is a good deal more important to keep people talking freedom in communist countries than to keep people talking communism out of this one.

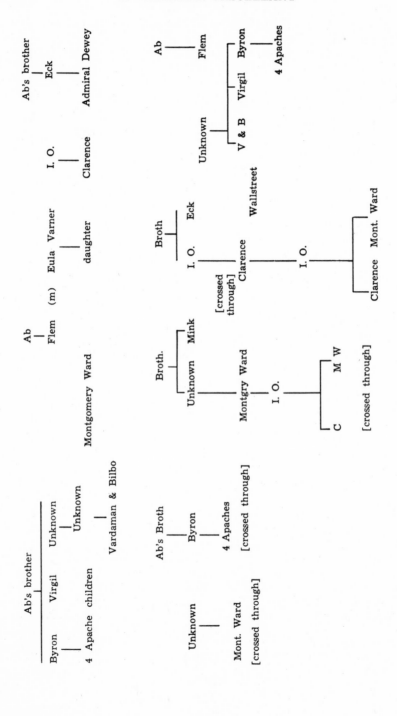

I was an air pilot since 1918 and a rated civilian one since about 1930.

I have done some work for the State Department, through junior career members——consuls, attaches, special officers——enough to have learned that the problems they have to cope with come not from the foreign countries they are sent to, but from their Washington headquarters.

Though I am 57 years old now, which means that for 7 years I have been realising that human beings dont really know very much about anything.

Yours truly,

[signature]
Wm Faulkner

4.

Unpublished letter to Mr. Flautt, in response to an article published in the Memphis *Commercial Appeal*, December 8, 1955 (sec. I, p. 1, cols. 6, 7; p. 8, col. 1). Verso of *Town* TS. p. [40]. The following typing errors have been emended:

line 15 alwasy] always
l. 17 neraly] nearly
l. 18 havetried] have tried
l. 34 qeuality] equality
l. 34 e ucation] education
l. 37 littel] little

This letter to Mr. Bob Flautt, president of the Lions Club of Glendora, Miss., refers to a resolution of that club condemning the shooting of Clinton Melton, a Negro filling station attendant, by Elmer Kimbell, a white cotton gin manager. The resolution describes Melton as "one of the finest members of the Negro race in this community." The portions of this resolution printed in the *Commercial Appeal* are as follows:

> "We intend to see to it that the forces of justice and right prevail in the wake of this woeful evil. . . .
> "We humbly confess in repentance for having so lived as a community that such an evil occurrence could happen. . . .
> "We consider the taking of the life of Clinton Melton an outrage against him, against all the people of Glendora, against the people of Mississippi, and against the entire human family."

Oxford, Miss.
8 Dec. 1955

Dear Mr Flautt:

I read with interest and respect quotes in this morning's Commercial Appeal from the Glendora Lions Club resolution regarding the filling station shooting.

I had in the mail this morning a letter from a Memphis Negro woman, unsigned, disagreeing with my stand on the Negro question in Mississippi, which she assumed to be a stand for complete integration. She said that my stand does harm to her people, keeps the bad ones in her race stirred up, that what the Negroes really want is to be let alone in segregation as it is, that the Negroes are against NAACP.

I have always believed that of some of our Negroes, what we call the 'best' Negroes. I have always said that the 'best' Negroes, I believe most, nearly all Negroes, do not want integration with white people any more than the best, nearly all, white people want integration with Negroes. What I have tried to say is, since there is much pressure today from outside our country to advance the Negro, let us here give the Negro a chance to prove whether he is or is not competent for educational and economic and political equality, before the Federal Government crams it down ours and the Negro's throat too. Then, if after the trial, the Negro does fail in being capable of equality with the federal government to back him, we in the South will have to cope not only with the failed Negro but the federal government too.

I believe that there are many more Negroes in the South like the woman who wrote me, who do not want integration but just justice, to be let alone by NAACP and all other disruptive forces, just freedom from threat of violence, etc. And I believe there are many more white people besides the members of your club, who are willing to see that the Negro is free from fear of violence and injustice and has freedom in which to prove whether or not he is competent for equality in education and economics and politics. I would like to think that if we could all work together ——the Negroes who do not want integration but simple justice and a little better life, and the white people like your club who are opposed to injustice and violence and outrage, no matter what color the victim is, we could handle this problem. We could indeed tell the federal government that we dont need it in our home affairs.

Yours sincerely,

[signature]
Wm Faulkner

5.

Unpublished letter to Mr. [W. C.] Neill, in reply to a copy of a letter of Neill to Congresswoman [Edith] Green which he had forwarded to Faulkner. Verso of *Town* TS. p. [80].

Mr. Neill (of North Carrollton, Miss.) was the author of an

earlier letter attacking Faulkner, which was published in the Memphis *Commercial Appeal*, March 27, 1955 (sec. V, p. 3, col. 4). Faulkner mentions in his essay "On Fear" (*ESPL*, pp. 93-94) a carbon copy of this public letter sent to him by Neill, in which Neill refers to him as "Weeping Willie." Faulkner's reply to Neill's public letter was published in the *Commercial Appeal*, April 3, 1955 (*ESPL*, pp. 218-219).

Oxford, Mississippi
Jan. 12, 1956

Dear Mr Neill:

My copy of your letter to Congresswoman Green was at hand when I reached home today.

Thank you for it, but I doubt if we can afford to waste even on Congress, let alone on one another, that wit which we will sorely need when again, for the second time in a hundred years, we Southerners will have destroyed our native land just because of niggers.

Yours truly

Wm Faulkner

cc: Congresswoman Bleeding Heart Green
      Fireball Frederick Sullens
      Hoochypap Henry Luce
      Holy Hodding Carter
      Weeping Willie Faulkner (kept his; saved three cents)

6.

Unpublished letter to the Secretary of the Junior Chamber of Commerce, Batesville, Miss. Verso of *Town* TS. p. [139].

A version of this letter was published in part in an article in the Memphis *Press-Scimitar*, August 11, 1956 (p. 11, col. 1). The article states that Faulkner's letter to the Chamber of Commerce accused the sheriff of Batesville of having had an informer who told that Mrs. Kayo McClamroch took a bottle of whiskey from wet Memphis to dry Mississippi. She was fined $125, and the citizens of Grenada County contributed money to repay her for the fine.

Oxford,
Lafayette Co.,
Miss.
Aug. 8, 1956

Secretary,
Junior Chamber of Commerce,
Batesville, Miss.

Dear Mr Secretary:
   Enclosed is my check for $1.00.
   Only a decade ago, we emerged from a terrible war in which
our nation gave of its blood and money both that the world be
freed of a tyranny founded on and supported by secret police and
their private informers.
   I am proud to be a citizen of a county having for neighbor
a county, a hundred of whose citizens have joined to resist and
repudiate this evil in our own land in which men and women can
still practice honor and freedom without risking both to do so,
of which the affair of Mrs McClamroch of Grenada, was a symp-
tom.
   My dollar is too late to be included in that group, but I hope
it is not too late for the tar-and-feathers fund for the brave and
honorable——and of course, naturally, nameless——patriot who re-
ported her.

                                        Yours truly,

                                        William Faulkner

                            7.

Unpublished letter to Mr. Colwell. Verso of *Mansion* TS.: chap.
6, p. 14.
The following errors have been emended:
11. 19-20 goverment] government
l. 33 Russinas] Russians
l. 36 hprses] horses

Dear Mr Colwell:
   I have pondered long and seriously over the invitation to
make one of a group of writers visiting Russia.
   I believe that for me to decline to visit Russia at present
would be of more value in the 'cold war' than my presence would.
   The Russia with which I would have spiritual kinship is the
Russia which produced Tolstoy, Dostoievsky, Chekov, Turgeniev,
Gogol, etc. It is no longer there. I dont mean it is dead; it will
take more than a police state to destroy the inheritors and practising
heirs of those men. I am convinced that they are still writing, at
the risk of life itself, hiding the mss. under floors, in chimneys,
against the day (which will come) when they too can be free
again.

   If by going to Russia under any condition, and even at the
risk or perhaps sacrifice (I am 60 now, have possibly done all
the good work I am capable of, was intended to do) of life, I
could free one Anna Kerenina or Brothers Karamazov, I would do
so.
   But to go there now, as a guest of the present Russian govern-

ment which, as I believe, has driven underground and would destroy them if it could, the heirs of the giants of the Russian spirit, the fact of even the outward appearance of condoning that condition would be a betrayal, not of the giants, nothing can harm them, but of their heirs who risk their lives with every page they write, but, which is worse, suffer the destruction of their souls in order to write and still remain alive

"but of both their true heirs . . ." who risk their lives to write even in secret, and of those who might have been their heirs who do worse: accept destruction of their souls for the privilege of writing in public

by me, who have had freedom in which to write truth as I saw it, of

I regret this. I have met a few Russians here and there, members of embassies and consulates. If they are a sample of the Russia today, they are   Among the frightened harassed mass of most of the rest of Western man, they stand out like horses standing in a pond seething with scared tadpoles. If they are a fair sample of the Russia today, all that saves us is Communism. If the Russians were free, they would probably conquer the earth.

8.

Letter to the Memphis *Commercial Appeal*, published in part September 15, 1957; cf. *ESPL*, p. 229. Versos of *Mansion* TS.: chap. 3, p. 2-B; chap. 6, p. 24.
The following error has been emended:
1. 13 priviledge] privilege

Faulkner refers to the letter of M. J. Greer, published in the *Commercial Appeal*, September 1, 1957 (sec. V, p. 3, col. 4). Greer states: "I only predict the end of LEGAL segregation. PERSONAL segregation, an entirely different aspect which extends beyond the racial phases, will be left to the individual's discretion, as it should be in a democracy."

To The Commercial Appeal:
The undersigned agrees with writer M. J. Greer (Letters to the Editor, Sept. 1st.) in his practical evaluation of the segregation problem. All the laws in the world will not make white and non-white people mix if one of the parties doesn't want to, just as all the laws in the world cant keep them separate if both parties want to mix.
I still dont believe the Negro wants to 'mix' with white people. I dont believe he likes white people that much. But, from three hundred years of association with white people, he has become enough like the white man to rebel at a culture which holds him inferior and second class simply because of his race and color——

which, because of his pigment, denies him privilege which anyone else with a different color of skin, possesses by natural right. He doesn't want to be in the white man's churches and schools anymore than he wants the white man in his: he simply wants the right to *choose* not to enter them.

A few years ago the Supreme Court rendered a decision which we white Southerners didn't like, and resisted. As a result, last month Congress would have passed a bill containing ramifications and implications a good deal more threatening than the presence of a Negro child in a white school or a Negro vote in a white ballot box, if there hadn't been one expert on hand to see it in time. So we escaped——that time. But as long as the Negro continues to be held inferior and second class in citizenship——that is, subject to taxes and military service, yet denied the economic and political and educational equality giving him at least the right and competence to vote for, even if not represented among, them who tax and draft him——Congress will continue to be offered bills containing these ramifications and implications visible only to an expert, until some day that expert wont be on hand to save us, and one of them will pass. But at least we will have the satisfaction of knowing that we have nobody to blame but ourselves.

If we really want to make admission to our schools selective and restrictive and still stay clear of Congress and the Supreme Court, all we need do is raise the standards of the grades and classes to that level where the schools themselves will exclude the inferior and the unfit——which we would have done long ago if we had wanted really to train and educate our children. But that would exclude some white pupils too so

9.

Letter to the *New York Times,* published in revised form October 13, 1957; cf. *ESPL,* p. 230. Verso of *Mansion* TS.: chap. 3, p. 5.

Editor,
New York TIMES,
New York, N. Y.

Sir:

The real tragedy of Little Rock is that it has brought out into the light a fact which both parties have managed to ignore by pretending it wasn't there. The Supreme Court, the N.A.A.C.P., Governor Faubus and President Eisenhower, all working together have brought out the fact that Negroes and whites simply do not like each other and probably will never trust one another; that since the Negro became free of the white man's agrarian economy, the two cultures have nothing in common save the in-

stallment-plan automobiles and radios and refrigerators, and perhaps never will have.

William Faulkner
Oxford, Miss.

10.

Three unpublished letters to the Memphis *Commercial Appeal,*
incorporated into the essay "On Fear: Deep South in Labor."
The first two of these letters, and perhaps the third, appear
to be attempts to reply to statements made by Faulkner's
brother John Faulkner in a letter to the *Commercial Appeal,*
December 4, 1955 (sec. IV, p. 3, cols. 7, 8). That letter of John
Faulkner is reprinted here in full, followed by the three unpublished letters of William Faulkner.

To THE Commercial Appeal:
One hundred years ago this country stood divided. Today
that same fact is true.

That first time the abolitionist societies drove the black wedge
of Negro equality between the North and South. Today the same
wedge has been used but it has assumed the shape of a sickle and
our own Supreme Court is the hammer that drove it home.

We are witnessing the living example of the oldest military
axiom: Divide and rule. It is strange to me that a man of Eisenhower's military perspicacity cannot or will not see this. It is
strange to me that men qualified to sit as the supreme arbiters
of our justice are so uninformed as to the people they sit in judgment on that they can believe that the South is any more ready
or willing to accept the Negro as an equal today than it was 100,
200 or 300 years ago.

If this be so, then they are certainly less well informed than
are the Russians, who did not bother to study our psychology in
efforts to divide us, but simply used the same effective weapon
that was used in 1861.

Communist gold supports the NAACP. This is of record. Our
Supreme Court hands down decisions based not on precedent which
is the basis of our system of justice but on the policies of the
NAACP, which is communist-supported.

Today the last voice against communism is that of the white
man of the South, and to raise his voice that white man is placed
as a political bedfellow with the Russians, for if two white men
speak against integration they have been judged in Federal court
to be in conspiracy against the United States Government and
therefore are subversives.

The most constant mouthings of the NAACP are that as we
resist integration, so we place a powerful weapon against us, as

far as the outside world is concerned, in the hands of the communists. Suppose we accept integration. Then we are communists,
for that is their credo.

The final step in communism is: No churches, for in their faith
the only religion must be the state; there is no place for God.
Even in Russia they have not yet dared to do away with the
churches. However, they have gone the next step to it: The state
has taken over control of church policy.

From The Commercial Appeal, Nov. 24, I hold this clipping:
"WASHINGTON, Nov. 23.— (AP) — Justice Department
sources said Wednesday the department's civil rights section
is 'studying' a Louisiana incident involving the reported re-
jection by a white congregation of the services of a Negro
Catholic priest."

I have noticed this: Of those white men of the South who mount
the platform to speak in favor of integration, I know a small few
personally. Of those I do know, not a single one is a member or
active communicant of any church.

JOHN FAULKNER
Oxford, Miss.

10 a.

Unpublished letter to the Memphis *Commercial Appeal*, incorporated into the essay "On Fear"; cf. *ESPL*, pp. 99-100.
Verso of *Town* TS. p. [29].

Oxford, Miss.
The Commercial Appeal: Dec. 5, 1955

Dear Sir:

I see in your correspondence of last Sunday that the threat of
communism and of atheism (agnosticism) are being used to defend
status quo segregation. All lacking of the old Hitler formula is
the threat of Semitism.

I dont remember ever seeing these three questions answered
by the proponents of status quo segregation:

1. Christianity says: There are no distinctions among men since
whosoever believeth in Me shall never die.
2. Morality says: Do unto others as you would have others do
unto you.
3. The Constitution of the U. S. says: Before the law, there shall
be no artificial inequality——creed race or money——among
citizens of the United States.

If these questions were answered, maybe all of us would be
on one side.   William Faulkner

10 b.

Unpublished letter to the Memphis *Commercial Appeal*, evident-

ly an expansion of the previous letter; cf. *ESPL*, pp. 98-100.
Versos of *Town* TS. pp. [48], [49].
The following errors have been emended.
1. 19 Southerns] Southerners
11. 22-23 perhape] perhaps

The Commercial Appeal:
　　During our trouble and indecision following the Supreme Court
ukase about segregation, we have heard many voices in Mississippi.
We have heard those of one of our United States senators and one
of our circuit judges, who, although they did not speak for the
Senate nor for the Bench, at least they made no attempt to conceal their identity and their condition.
　　We have heard the voices of citizens who, although they did
not speak specifically for the white Citizens' Councils nor for the
NAACP, neither did they attempt to conceal their identity and
convictions. We have heard the voices of our schoolmen, teachers
and pupils, even though they could not always risk signing their
names to their letters.
　　But there is one voice which we have not heard: that voice
which should have adumbrated to silence all the other voices since
it is superior to all, being the living articulation of the glory and
sovereignty of God and of the hope and aspiration of man. The
Church, which is the strongest unified force in our Southern life,
since all Southerners are not white and all Southerners are not
democrats but all Southerners are religious and all religions serve
the same single God, no matter by what name He is known.
　　Where is that voice now, which should have propounded perhaps two but certainly one of these still-unanswered questions?
1.　The Constitution of the U. S. says: Before the law, there shall
　　be no artificial inequality——race creed or money——among
　　citizens of the United States.
2.　Morality says: Do unto others as you would have others do
　　unto you.
3.　Christianity says: I am the only distinction among men since
　　whosoever believeth in Me, shall never die.
　　Where is this voice now? Is it trying to tell us by its silence
that it wants no part of our troubles when perhaps all we need
is the simple voice of God?
　　　　　　　　　　　　William Faulkner
　　　　　　　　　　　　Oxford, Miss.

10 c.

Unpublished letter to the Memphis *Commercial Appeal*, incorporated into the essay "On Fear"; cf. *ESPL*, pp. 97-98.
Versos of *Town* TS. pp. [31], [32], [36].

The following error has been emended:
1. 3 ninettenth] nineteenth

The Commercial Appeal

Dear Sir:

In the first half of the nineteenth century, before slavery was abolished by law in the United States, Thomas Jefferson and Abraham Lincoln both held that the Negro was not yet competent for equality.

That was more than ninety years ago though, and nobody can say whether their opinions would be different now or not.

But assume that they would not have changed their belief, and that that opinion is right. Assume that the Negro is still not competent for equality, which is something which neither he nor the white man knows until we try it.

But we do know that, with the support of the federal government, the Negro is going to gain the right to try and see if he is fit or not for equality. And if we cannot trust him with something as mild as equality given him voluntarily as a free gift, what will we do when he has power——the power of victory in his right to test his capacity for equality, compelled by the federal government: stop him? this, when the only check on that power will be the federal government which is already his ally?

In 1849 John C. Calhoun made his address in favor of secession if the Wilmot Proviso was ever adopted. On Oct. 12th of that year, Senator Jefferson Davis wrote a public letter to the South, saying: "the generation which avoids its responsibility on this subject sows the wind and leaves the whirlwind as a harvest to its children. Let us get together and build manufactures, enter upon industrial pursuits, and prepare for our own self-sustenance."

At that time the Constitution guaranteed the Negro as property along with all other property, and Senator Calhoun and Senator Davis had the then undisputed validity of States' Rights to back their position. Now the Constitution guarantees the Negro equal right to equality, and states' rights do not exist anymore. We——the South——sold our states rights back to the federal government when we accepted the first cotton price-support subsidy about twenty years ago. Our economy is not agriculture anymore. It is the Federal Government. We no longer farm in Mississippi fields. We farm in Washington corridors and Congressional committee-rooms.

We——the South——didn't heed Senator Davis' words then. But let us heed them now. If we are to watch our native land wrecked and ruined twice in less than a hundred years by the Negro question, let us be sure this time we know where we are going afterward.

William Faulkner
Oxford, Miss.

JAMES B. MERIWETHER
University of South Carolina

William Faulkner's Own Collection of His Books in 1959

IN JOSEPH BLOTNER's very useful compilation, *William Faulkner's Library—A Catalogue* (Charlottesville, 1964), very few of Faulkner's own books are listed. In September 1962 (only two months after Faulkner's death) Professor Blotner went through the books in Rowanoak, Faulkner's house in Oxford, Mississippi. At that time he found only a few books by Faulkner in the library: the 1950 *Collected Stories*, the 1951 Modern Library reissue of *Absalom, Absalom!*, the 1947 Continental Book Co. (Sweden) edition of *Sanctuary*, and the 1942 English edition of *Go Down, Moses*. In Faulkner's study were three collections of his early work edited by others: *Mirrors of Chartres Street* (1953), *New Orleans Sketches* (1961 paperback reissue), and *Early Prose and Poetry* (1962).[1]

In the introduction to the catalogue, Professor Blotner states that most of Faulkner's own books at Rowanoak "stayed in a special bookcase he never bothered with. When a new volume arrived, he would give it to Mrs. Faulkner, who would unlock the bookcase and place it with its predecessors. These I have not listed." On January 24, 1959, I visited Faulkner at Rowanoak, where he was finishing the writing of *The Mansion*. I asked him a number of bibliographical questions about his writings, and at

---

[1] Something appears to be amiss here; Carvel Collins' edition of the *Early Prose and Poetry* (Boston: Little, Brown, 1962) was published in November and could hardly have got into Faulkner's study shelves by September 1962. Presumably it was sent by editor or publisher, got put on the shelf by someone else, and got included in the Blotner catalogue in the checking or proof stages of the compilation. It does give the impression of belonging with the other group in the study, though it is difficult to imagine Faulkner, who had no copy of his own books in his study, wanting to have there these compilations of the early work which he wanted ignored. Did he stick them there simply to keep them out of sight?

one point he suggested that I might want to examine the copies of his books in the case on the south wall of the library, which he unlocked for me, apologising, as he did so, that I would not find all of them—he had no copy at all, he said, of a good many of his books.

At the time I took notes on those of his books which he did have in that case. After his death they were moved to Knole Farm, near Charlottesville, by his daughter, Mrs Paul D. Summers, Jr., who very kindly permitted me to take another look at several of them, in January 1968 and July 1973, to check my notes. It seems worthwhile now to describe those books, as a supplement to the Blotner catalogue, and as an indication of which of his books he actually had available to him at Rowanoak, at that point in his career.

Absalom, Absalom!
1. New York: Random House, 1936. 2nd printing. Signed on fly-leaf and title-page.
2. Another copy (also 2nd printing).
3 & 4. London: Chatto and Windus, 1937. The first impression of the first English issue. 2 copies, in jackets, as issued: printed flaps, rest clear plastic.

As I Lay Dying
1. New York: Cape and Smith, 1930. 2nd state (initial "I" out of line, p. 11) of first printing. Picture of Faulkner from a periodical pasted inside front cover.

Doctor Martino and Other Stories
1. New York: Smith and Haas, 1934. First (and only American) printing. Signed on title-page: "William Faulkner / Oxford, / 16 April, 1934" (publication date was April 16). Inscribed on fly-leaf: "For my mother, with love. Billy".

Go Down, Moses
1 & 2. New York: Random House, 1942. First binding (black cloth, top edges stained red) of first printing. 2 copies, in dust jackets.

Notes on a Horsethief
1 & 2. Greenville, Miss.: Levee Press, 1951. 2 copies, out-of-series (unnumbered and unsigned).

Pylon
1. London: Chatto & Windus, 1935. Centaur Library reissue, apparently from sheets of the first English impression. Dust jacket has

Centaur Library label pasted on spine. (I described this copy in greater detail in *The Literary Career of William Faulkner,* Princeton, 1961, p. 107.)

Sanctuary

1. London: Chatto and Windus, 1933. First printing of the Phoenix Library issue of the first English edition.

The Unvanquished

1. Leipzig: Albatross Verlag, 1938. Apparently first impression of this English-language continental edition. Stiff wrappers, with paper dust jacket.[2]

JAMES B. MERIWETHER

University of South Carolina

---

[2] Faulkner, observing me studying this book with some care (I had not seen a copy before), asked me why I was so interested in it. I told him that I was trying to determine the exact color of the wrappers. He took the book from me, gave it a single sharp glance, and handed it back with the comment, "That's what painters call Portuguese Pink."

NOEL POLK

University of Texas at Arlington

"Hong Li" and *Royal Street:*

The New Orleans Sketches in Manuscript

DURING THE 1920's William Faulkner wrote and "published" a series of hand-printed, hand-decorated, and hand-bound manuscript pamphlets, for distribution to friends. Carvel Collins has called attention to three of them—*Marionettes* (of which Faulkner made more than one copy), *Mayday,* and *The Lilacs*[1] —and, according to information supplied with its publication in 1967 by Random House, a small typescript of *The Wishing Tree* was also bound in this manner, in 1927. Recently another such booklet has been added to the Faulkner collection at the University of Texas. Its title page transcribes: "ROYAL STREET | NEW ORLEANS | WILLIAM FAULKNER," and in it Faulkner reproduces by hand, in slightly revised texts, all but one of the eleven short pieces which he had published under the collective title "New Orleans" in the January-February 1925 issue of *The Double Dealer,* and which Collins included in his 1968 *New Orleans Sketches.*

Royal Street is a small but handsomely bound pamphlet; it has 26 pages and measures 6 ½" x 5 3/16". The front end-paper is decorated with an inkdrawing, like that in *Marionettes,* after Beardsley, and the first letter of each sketch is elaborately decorated, in large blocks, and colored, like a medieval illuminated manuscript. It is dedicated "To Estelle, a | Lady, with | Respectful Admiration: | This," and the verso of the dedication page reads: "Acknowledgments to 'The Double Dealer' | single mss. impression——Oxford——Mississippi——29 October 1926."

---

[1] Collins, ed., *Early Prose and Poetry* (Boston, 1962), pp. 11-13, 18; Collins, ed., *New Orleans Sketches* (New York, 1968), pp. xiii-xiv, xxx. For further discussion of *Marionettes* see Michael Millgate, *The Achievement of William Faulkner* (New York, 1966), pp. 8-9; James B. Meriwether's *The Literary Career of William Faulkner* (Princeton, 1961; reissue, Columbia, S. C., 1971), pp. 8-9 and Figure 1; and my own article "William Faulkner's *Marionettes"* elsewhere in this issue of *Mississippi Quarterly.*

One *Double Dealer* sketch, "The Tourist," is not included in *Royal Street*, but Faulkner offsets its lack by the inclusion of a new one, entitled "Hong Li," the text of which is printed below. I am grateful to Mrs. Jill Faulkner Summers, Faulkner's daughter and literary executrix, for permission to reproduce the text of "Hong Li." I would also like to thank the Committee on the Use of Historical and Literary Manuscripts at the University of Texas for allowing me access to the Texas Manuscript Collections.

HONG LI*

It is written that a man's senses are as bees which, while hiving the indiscriminate honey of his days, cement unawares the imperishable edifice of his soul. What matter if at times the honey seem oversweet to him, or seem to his inferior clay, bitter even? The honey's sweetness is but comparative: soon sweet becomes pallid and without taste; oversweet, but sweet; and at last bitterness strikes no responding chord and man is as a gorged reptile supine before the croaching rumor of worms.

Misfortune is man's greatest gift: happiness is as the orchid that rots the trunk to which it clings and which, removed, dies, leaving the soul a battened pig grunting and jaded in its own filth. Sorrow purges it, and the soul is as the imperishable willow, grave without sadness nor desire. Bereavement? a thing for unlettered beasts to lift yowling inarticulate faces to the remote contemplation of Cosmos. Bereavement of woman, of a little parcel of scented flesh, an articulation of minute worms? Beasts yowling for beasts in the accumulate mud of Time. But for one of the fourth degree? Heh!

The husbandman winnows his grain ere he sow it; the wise husbandman destroys the seed of tares. So do I, in the nurtured garden of my soul, winnow carefully the grain given me; so do I root out and destroy the tares which her dead and delicate feet sowed across my heart, that my soul may be as a garden beyond the rumors of the world for the contemplation of the evening of my life. For it is written that sorrow is as the fire in which the sword is tempered, but that despair is an attribute of beasts.

But Ehee, Ehee, her little little feet.

And Now What's To Do

[*The two-page manuscript of this unfinished piece by Faulkner turned up with the group of his papers that were found in 1970 in a closet at Rowanoak. Although it cannot now be dated precisely, it was apparently written sometime during the latter part of the 1920's, perhaps between 1925, when his writing first began showing the influence of Sherwood Anderson, and about 1927 or 1928.*

The most unusual feature of the piece is its very clear autobiographical element. Faulkner may have intended it for a short story, and not everything in it should be taken literally, but in the part he completed he drew upon his own life to a greater extent than he did in any piece of fiction he ever wrote. Not until a quarter of a century later, in the semi-fictional essay "Mississippi," did he again so obviously center a piece of writing on his own experiences.

A few editorial changes have been necessary. Faulkner's period after the title was omitted. At line oo a period has been substituted for a semicolon which Faulkner forgot to change when he cancelled a long passage following. And five abbreviations have been expanded in accordance with Faulkner's own practice when he typed out his manuscripts: 400.3, Xmas] Christmas; 400.31, 18] eighteen; 400.32, 3] three; 400.34, 20] twenty; 400.35, 30] thirty. —J. B.M.]

His great-grandfather came into the country afoot from the Tennessee mountains, where he had killed a man, worked and saved and bought a little land, won a little more at cards and dice, and died at the point of a pistol while trying to legislate himself into a little more; his grandfather was a deaf, upright man in white linen, who wasted his inherited substance in politics. He had a law practice still, but he sat most of the day in the courthouse yard, a brooding, thwarted old man too deaf to take part in conversation and whom the veriest child could beat at checkers. His father loved horses better than books or learning; he owned a livery stable, and here the boy grew up, impregnated with the violent ammoniac odor of horses. At ten he could stand on a box and harness a horse and put it between runabout shafts almost as quickly as a grown man, darting beneath its belly like a cricket to buckle the straps, cursing it in his shrill cricket voice; by the time he was twelve he had acquired from the negro hostlers an uncanny skill with a pair of dice.

Each Christmas eve his father carried a hamper full of whisky in pint bottles to the stable and stood with it in the office door, against the firelight, while the negroes gathered and rolled their eyes and ducked their gleaming teeth in the barn cavern, filled with snorts and stampings of contentment. The boy, become adolescent, helped to drink this; old ladies smelled his breath at times and tried to save his soul. Then he was sixteen and he began to acquire a sort of inferiority complex regarding his father's business. He had gone through grammar school and one year in high school with girls and boys (on rainy days, in a hack furnished by his father he drove about the neighborhood and gathered up all it would hold free of charge) whose fathers were lawyers and doctors and merchants ——all genteel professions, with starched collars. He had been unselfconscious then, accepting all means of earning bread as incidental to following whatever occupation a man preferred. But not now. All this was changed by his changing body. Before and during puberty he learned about women from the negro hostlers and the white night-man, by listening to their talk. Now, on the street, he looked after the same girls he had once taken to school in his father's hack, watching their forming legs, imagining their blossoming thighs, with a feeling of defiant inferiority. There was a giant in him, but the giant was muscle-bound. The boys, the doctors' and merchants' and lawyers' sons, loafed on the corners before the drug stores. None of them could make a pair of dice behave as he could.

An automobile came to town. The horses watched it with swirling proud eyes and tossing snorts of alarm. The war came, a sound afar off heard. He was eighteen, he had not been in school since three years; the moth-eaten hack rusted quietly among the jimson weeds in the stable yard. He no longer smelled of ammonia, for he could now win twenty or thirty dollars any Sunday in the crap game in the wooded park near the railway station; and on the drug store corner where the girls passed in soft troops, touching one another with their hands and with their arms you could not tell him from a lawyer's or a merchant's or a doctor's son. The girls didn't, with their ripening thighs and their mouths that keep you awake at night with unnameable things——shame of lost integrity, manhood's pride, desire like a drug. The body is tarnished, soiled in its pride, now. But what is it for, anyway?

A girl got in trouble, and he clung to boxcar ladders or lay in empty gondolas while railjoints clicked under the cold stars. Frost had not yet fallen upon the cotton, but it had touched the gum-lined Kentucky roads and the broad grazing lands, and lay upon the shocked corn of Ohio farm land beneath the moon. He lay on his back in an Ohio hay stack. The warm dry hay was about his legs. It had soaked a summer's sun, and it held him suspended in dry and sibilant warmth where he moved unsleeping, cradling his head, thinking of home. Girls were all right, but there were so many girls everywhere. So many of them a man had to get through with in the world, politely. It meant tactfully. Nothing to girls. Dividing legs dividing receptive. He had known all about it before, but the reality was like reading a story and then seeing it in the movies, with music and all. Soft things. Secretive, but like traps. Like going after something you wanted, and getting into a nest of spider webs. You got the thing, then you had to pick the webs off, and every time you touched one, it stuck to you. Even after you didn't want the thing anymore, the webs clung to you. Until after a while you remembered the way the webs itched and you wanted the thing again, just thinking of how the webs itched. No. Quicksand. That was it. Wade through once, then go on. But a man wont. He wants to go all the way through, somehow; break out on the other side. Everything incomplete somehow. Having to back off, with webs clinging to you. "Christ, you have to tell them so much. You cant think of it fast enough. And they never forget when you do and when you dont. What do they want, anyway?"

Across the moon a V of geese slid, their lonely cries drifted in the light of chill and haughty stars across the shocked corn and the supine delivered earth, lonely and sad and wild. Winter: season of sin and death. The geese were going south, but his direction was steadily north. In an Ohio town one night, in a saloon, he got to know a man who was travelling from county seat to county seat with a pacing horse, making the county fairs. The man was cunning in a cravatless collar, lachrymosely panegyric of the pacing of the horse; and together they drifted south again and again his garments became impregnated with ammonia. Horses smelled good again, rankly ammoniac, with their ears like frost-touched vine leaves [.]

Nympholepsy

[*In 1922 Faulkner published a prose sketch entitled "The Hill"
in* The Mississippian, *the undergraduate newspaper of the University
of Mississippi. Along with the unpublished play "The
Marionettes," it was the most accomplished and ambitious piece of
writing he attempted before he undertook his first novel,* Soldiers'
Pay, *in the spring of 1925. The oddly-entitled "Nympholepsy" is
an expansion of "The Hill," which Faulkner apparently wrote
early in 1925, within the first month or two of his arrival in New
Orleans. The text here is taken from the eight-page typescript at
the Henry W. and Albert A. Berg Collection of the New York
Public Library (Astor, Lenox and Tilden Foundations). I am indebted
to Mme. Lola Szladits, Curator of the Berg Collection, for
making it possible to publish it here.*

*The following typing errors have been corrected: 404.2, yoing]
young; 404.11, awayl] away; 405.25, abarn] a barn; 406.10, uopn
] upon; 406.31, imminet] imminent; 406.33, is] it; 406.36, intergral
] integral; 407.5, felling] feeling; 407.11, derisove] derisive;
407.25, rippels] ripples; 408.34, He] His; 408.37, hw] he;
409.4, he] He; 409.16, sinsister] sinister.—J. B. M.*]

Soon the sharp line of the hill-crest had cut off his shadow's
head; and pushing it like a snake before him, he saw it gradually
become nothing. And at last he had no shadow at all. His
heavy shapeless shoes were gray in the dusty road, his overalls
were gray with dust: dust was like a benediction upon him
and upon the day of labor behind him. He did not recall the
falling of slain wheat and his muscles had forgotten the heave
and thrust of fork and grain, his hands had forgotten the feel
of a wooden handle worn smoothe and sweet as silk to the touch;
he had forgotten a yawning loft and spinning chaff in the sunlight like an immortal dance.

Behind him a day of labor, before him cloddish eating, and
dull sleep in a casual rooming house. And tomorrow labor again
and his sinister circling shadow marking another day away.
The hill broke briefly and sharply, soon, on its crest it was no
more sharp. Here was the valley in shadow, and the opposite
hill in two dimensions and gold with sun. Within the valley
the town lay among lilac shadows. Among lilac shadows was
the food he would eat and the sleep that waited him; perhaps
a girl like defunctive music, moist with heat, in blue gingham,

would cross his path fatefully; and he too would be as other young men sweating the wheat to gold, along the moony land.

Here was town anyway. Above gray walls were branches of apple once sweet with bloom and yet green, barn and house were hives from which the bees of sunlight had flown away. From here the court-house was a dream dreamed by Thucydides: you could not see that pale Ionic columns were stained with casual tobacco. And from the blacksmith's there came the measured ring of hammer and anvil like a call to vespers.

Reft of motion, his body felt his cooling blood, felt the evening drawing away like water; his eyes saw the shadow of the church spire like a portent across the land. He watched the trickling dust from his inverted shoes. His feet were grained and grimy with dust; and cooled, took the pleasantly warm moistness of his shoes gratefully.

The sun was a red descending furnace mouth, his shadow he had thought lost crouched like a skulking dog at his feet. The sun was in the trees, dripping from leaf to leaf, the sun was like a little silver flame moving among the trees. Why, its something alive, he thought, watching a golden light among dark pines, a little flame that had somehow lost its candle and was seeking for it.

How he knew it was a woman or a girl at that distance he could not have told, but know he did; and for a time he watched the aimless movements of the figure with vacuous curiosity. The figure, pausing, took the last of the red sun in a slim golden plane that, breaking again into movement, disappeared.

For a clear moment there was an old sharp beauty behind his eyes. Then his once-clean instincts become swinish got him lurching into motion. He climbed a fence under the contemplative stare of cattle and ran awkwardly across a harvested corn field toward the woods. Old soft furrows shifted beneath his stride, causing his pounding knees to knock together and brittle corn stalks hindered his speed with wanton and static unconcern.

He gained the woods by climbing another fence and stopped for a moment while the west alchemized the leaden dust upon him, gilding the tips of his unshaven beard. Hardwood,——maple and beech trunks, were twin strips of red gold and lavender upright in earth, and stretched branches sloped the sunset to unwordable colors;——they were like the hands of misers reluctantly dripping golden coins of sunset. Pines were half iron and half bronze, sculptured into a symbol of eternal quiet, dripping gold also which the sparse grass took from tree to tree like a running fire, quenching it at last in the shadow of pines. A bird on a swinging branch regarded him briefly, sung, and flew away.

Before this green cathedral of trees he stood for a while, empty as a sheep, feeling the dying day draining from the world as a bath-tub drains, or a cracked bowl; and he could hear the day repeating slow orisons in a green nave. Then he moved forward again, slowly, as though he expected a priest to stop forth, halting him and reading his soul.

Nothing happened though. The day slowly died without a sound about him, and gravity directed him down hill along peaceful avenues of trees. Soon the violet shadow of the hill itself took him. There was no sun here, though the tips of trees were still as gold-dipped brushes and the trunks of trees upon the summit were like a barred grate beyond which the evening burned slowly away. He stopped again, knowing fear.

He recalled fragments of the day——of sucking cool water from a jug with another waiting his turn, of the wheat breaking to the reaper's blade as the thrusting horses surged to the collar, of horses dreaming of oats in a barn sweet with ammonia and the smell of sweaty harness, of blackbirds like scraps of burned paper slanting above the wheat. He thought of the run of muscles beneath a blue shirt wet with sweat, and of someone to listen or talk to. Always someone, some other member of his race, of his kind. Man can counterfeit everything except silence. And in this silence he knew fear.

For here was something that even the desire for a woman's body took no account of. Or, using that instinct for the purpose of seducing him from the avenues of safety, of security where others of his kind ate and slept, it had betrayed him. If I find her, I am safe he thought, not knowing whether it was copulation or companionship that he wanted. There was nothing here for him: hills, sloping down on either side, approaching yet forever severed by a small stream. The water ran brown under

alders and willow, and without light, seemed dark and for-
bidding. Like the hand of the world, like a line on the palm
of the world's hand———a wrinkle of no account. Yet he could
drown here! he thought with terror, watching the spinning
gnats above it and the trees calm and uncaring as gods, and the
remote sky like a silken pall to hide his unsightly dissolution.

He had thought of trees as being so much timber but these
silent ones were more than that. Timber had made houses to
shelter him, timber had fed his fire for warmth, had given him
heat to cook his food; timber had made him boats to go upon
the waters of the earth. But not these trees. These trees gazed
on him impersonally, taking a slow revenge. The sunset was a
fire no fuel had ever fed, the water murmured in a dark and
sinister dream. No boat would swim on this water. And above
all brooded some god to whose compulsions he must answer
long after the more comfortable beliefs had become out-worn
as a garment used everyday.

And this god neither recognised him nor ignored him: this
god seemed to be unconscious of his entity, save as a trespasser
where he had no business being. Crouching, he felt the sharp
warm earth against his knees and his palms; and kneeling, he
awaited abrupt and dreadful annihilation.

Nothing happened, and he opened his eyes. Above the hill-
crest, among tree trunks, he saw a single star. It was as though
he had seen a man there. Here was a familiar thing, something
too remote to care what he did. So he rose and with the star
at his back, he began walking swiftly in the direction of town.
Here was the stream to cross. The delay of looking for a crossing
place engendered again his fear. But he suppressed it by his
will, thinking of food and of a woman he hoped to find.

That sensation of an imminent displeasure and anger, of a
Being whom he had offended, he held away from himself. But
it still hung like poised wings about and above him. His first
fear was gone, but soon he found himself running. He would
have slowed to a walk if only to prove to himself the soundness
of his integral integrity, but his legs would not stop running.
Here, in the noncommittal dusk, was a log bridging the stream.
Walk it! walk it! his good sense told him; but his thrusting legs
took it at a run.

The rotten bark slipped under his feet, scaling off and falling upon the dark whispering stream. It was as though he stood upon the bank and cursed his blundering body as it slipped and fought for balance. You are going to die, he told his body, feeling that imminent Presence again about him, now that his mental concentration had been vanquished by gravity. For an arrested fragment of time he felt, through vision without intellect, the waiting dark water, the treacherous log, the tree trunks pulsing and breathing and the branches like an invocation to a dark and unseen god; then trees and the star-flown sky slowly arced across his eyes. In his fall was death, and a bleak derisive laughter. He died time and again, but his body refused to die. Then the water took him.

Then the water took him. But here was something more than water. The water ran darkly between his body and his overalls and shirt, he felt his hair lap backward wetly. But here beneath his hand a startled thigh slid like a snake, among dark bubbles he felt a swift leg; and, sinking, the point of a breast scraped his back. Amid a slow commotion of disturbed water he saw death like a woman shining and drowned and waiting, saw a flashing body tortured by water; and his lungs spewing water gulped wet air.

Churned water lapped at his mouth, trying to enter, and the light of day prisoned beneath the stream broke again upon the surface, shaped to ripples. Gleaming planes of light angled and broke the surface, moving away from him; and treading water, feeling his sodden shoes and his heavy overalls, feeling his wet hair plastered upon his face, he saw her swing herself, dripping, up the bank.

He churned the water in pursuit. It seemed that he would never reach the other side. His heavy water-soaked clothes clung to him like importunate sirens, like women; he saw the broken water of his endeavor crested with stars. Finally he was in the shadow of willows and felt wet and slippery earth under his hand. Here was a root, and here a branch. He drew himself up, hearing the trickling water from his clothing, feeling his clothing become light and then heavy.

His shoes squashed limply and his clinging nondescript garments hampered his running, heavily. He could see her body, ghostly in the moonless dusk, mounting the hill. And he ran, cursing, with water dripping from his hair, with his coarse clothing and shoes wetly complaining, cursing his fate and his luck. He believed he could do better without the shoes, so, still watching the muted flame of her running, he removed them, then he took up the pursuit again. His wet clothes were like lead, he was panting when he crested the hill. There she was, in a wheat field under the rising harvest moon, like a ship on a silver sea.

He plunged after her. His furrow broke silver in the wheat beneath the impervious moon, rippling away from him, dying again into the dull and unravished gold of standing grain. She was far ahead, the disturbance of her passage through the wheat had died away ere he reached it. He saw, beyond the spreading ripple of her passage arcing away on either side, her body break briefly against a belt of wood, like a match flame; then he saw her no more.

Still running, he crossed the wheat slumbrous along the moony land, and into the trees he went, wearily. But she was gone, and in a recurrent surge of despair he threw himself flat upon the earth. But I touched her! he thought in a fine agony of disappointment, feeling the earth through his damp clothing, feeling twigs beneath his face and arm.

The moon swam up, the moon sailed up like a fat laden ship before an azure trade wind, staring at him in rotund complacency. He writhed, thinking of her body beneath his, of the dark wood, of the sunset and the dusty road, wishing he had never left it. But I touched her! he repeated to himself, trying to build from this an incontrovertible consummation. Yes, her swift frightened thigh and the tip of her breast; but to remember that she had fled him on impulse was worse than ever. I wouldnt have hurt you, he moaned, I wouldnt have hurt you at all.

His lax muscles, emptied, felt a rumor of past labor and of labor tomorrow, compulsions of fork and grain. The moon soothed him, prying in his wet hair, experimenting with shadows; and thinking of tomorrow he rose. That troubling Presence was gone and dark and shadows only mocked him.

The moonlight ran along a wire fence and he knew that here was the road.

He felt the dust stirring to his passage and he saw silver corn in fields, and dark trees like poured ink. He thought of how like running quicksilver she had looked, how like a flipped coin she had sped from him; but soon the lights of town came into view———the courthouse clock, and a luminous suggestion of streets, like a fairy land, small though it was. Soon she was forgotten and he thought only a relaxed body in a sorry bed, and waking and hunger and work.

The long monotonous road stretched under the moon before him. Now his shadow was behind him, like a following dog, and beyond it was a day of labor and sweat. Before him was sleep and casual food and more labor; and perhaps a girl like defunctive music, in this calico against the heat. Tomorrow his sinister shadow would circle him again, but tomorrow was a long way off.

The moon swam higher and higher: soon she would slide down the hill of heaven, recalling with interest the silver she had lent to tree and wheat and hill and rolling monotonous fecund land. Below him a barn took the moon for a silver edge and a silo became a dream dreamed in Greece, apple trees broke into silver like gesturing fountains. Flat planes of moonlight the town, and the lights on the courthouse were futile in the moon.

Behind him labor, before him labor; about all the old despairs of time and breath. The stars were like shattered flowers floating on dark water, sucking down the west; and with dust clinging to his yet damp feet, he slowly descended the hill.

An Introduction to *The Sound And The Fury*

[*For a new edition of* The Sound and the Fury *that was to be published by Random House, Faulkner wrote, during the summer of 1933, an introduction that survives in several partial and complete manuscript and typescript drafts. One of them, apparently the last, was published in the* SOUTHERN REVIEW, 8 *(N.S., Autumn 1972), 705-710. The following longer and quite different version also merits publication in its own right, and it is at least possible that it was written later, rather than earlier, than the one that has been published.*

The following typing or spelling errors have been corrected: 410.6, bourgoise] bourgeois; 410.9, grils] girls; 410.11, lynotype] linotype; 410.14, polititians] politicians; 410.15, indians] Indians; 410.19, the] then; 411.11, typewritter] typewriter; 412.5, enviroment] environment; 412.16, one] ones; 412.16, writes] write; 412.32, trird] third; 413.1, threee] three; 413.25, leacened] leavened; 415.1, ardously] arduously; 415.17, writting] writing; 415.22, april] April.*—J. B. M.*]

Art is no part of southern life. In the North it seems to be different. It is the hardest minor stone in Manhattan's foundation. It is a part of the glitter or shabbiness of the streets. The arrowing buildings rise out of it and because of it, to be torn down and arrow again. There will be people leading small bourgeois lives (those countless and almost invisible bones of its articulation, lacking any one of which the whole skeleton might collapse) whose bread will derive from it——polyglot boys and girls progressing from tenement schools to editorial rooms and art galleries; men with grey hair and paunches who run linotype machines and take up tickets at concerts and then go sedately home to Brooklyn and suburban stations where children and grandchildren await them——long after the descendents of Irish politicians and Neapolitan racketeers are as forgotten as the wild Indians and the pigeon.

And of Chicago too: of that rythm not always with harmony or tune; lusty, loudvoiced, always changing and always young; drawing from a river basin which is almost a continent young men and women into its living unrest and then spewing them

---

forth again to write Chicago in New England and Virginia and
Europe. But in the South art, to become visible at all, must
become a ceremony, a spectacle; something between a gypsy
encampment and a church bazaar given by a handful of alien
mummers who must waste themselves in protest and active self-
defense until there is nothing left with which to speak——a
single week, say, of furious endeavor for a show to be held on
Friday night and then struck and vanished, leaving only a paint-
stiffened smock or a worn out typewriter ribbon in the corner
and perhaps a small bill for cheesecloth or bunting in the hands
of an astonished and bewildered tradesman.

"Perhaps this is because the South (I speak in the sense of
the indigenous dream of any given collection of men having
something in common, be it only geography and climate, which
shape their economic and spiritual aspirations into cities, into
a pattern of houses or behavior) is old since dead. New York,
whatever it may believe of itself, is young since alive; it is still
a logical and unbroken progression from the Dutch. And Chicago
even boasts of being young. "But the South, as Chicago is the
Middlewest and New York the East, is dead, killed by the Civil
War. There is a thing known whimsically as the New South
to be sure, but it is not the south. It is a land of Immigrants who
are rebuilding the towns and cities into replicas of towns and
cities in Kansas and Iowa and Illinois, with skyscrapers and
striped canvas awnings instead of wooden balconies, and teach-
ing the young men who sell the gasoline and the waitresses in
the restaurants to say O yeah? and to speak with hard r's, and
hanging over the intersections of quiet and shaded streets where
no one save Northern tourists in Cadillacs and Lincolns ever pass
at a gait faster than a horse trots, changing red-and-green lights
and savage and peremptory bells. "

Yet this art, which has no place in southern life, is almost
the sum total of the Southern artist. It is his breath, blood,
flesh, all. Not so much that it is forced back upon him or that
he is forced bodily into it by the circumstance; forced to choose,
lady and tiger fashion, between being an artist and being a man.
He does it deliberately; he wishes it so. This has always been
true of him and of him alone. Only Southerners have taken
horsewhips and pistols to editors about the treatment or mal-

treatment of their manuscript. This——the actual pistols—— was in the old days, of course, we no longer succumb to the impulse. But it is still there, still within us.

" Because it is himself that the Southerner is writing about, not about his environment: who has, figuratively speaking, taken the artist in him in one hand and his milieu in the other and thrust the one into the other like a clawing and spitting cat into a croker sack. And he writes. We have never got and probably will never get, anywhere with music or the plastic forms. We need to talk, to tell, since oratory is our heritage. We seem to try in the simple furious breathing (or writing) span of the individual to draw a savage indictment of the con- temporary scene or to escape from it into a makebelieve region of swords and magnolias and mockingbirds which perhaps never existed anywhere. Both of the courses are rooted in sentiment; perhaps the ones who write savagely and bitterly of the incest in clayfloored cabins are the most sentimental. Anyway, each course is a matter of violent partizanship, in which the writer unconsciously writes into every line and phrase his violent despairs and rages and frustrations or his violent prophesies of still more violent hopes. That cold intellect which can write with calm and complete detachment and gusto of its contempo- rary scene is not among us; I do not believe there lives the Southern writer who can say without lying that writing is any fun to him. Perhaps we do not want it to be.

I seem to have tried both of the courses. I have tried to escape and I have tried to indict. After five years I look back at *The Sound and The Fury* and see that that was the turning point: in this book I did both at one time. When I began the book, I had no plan at all. I wasn't even writing a book. Previous to it I had written three novels, with progressively decreasing ease and pleasure, and reward or emolument. The third one was shopped about for three years during which I sent it from publisher to publisher with a kind of stubborn and fading hope of at least justifying the paper I had used and the time I had spent writing it. This hope must have died at last, because one day it suddenly seemed as if a door had clapped silently and forever to between me and all publishers' addresses and booklists and I said to myself, Now I can write. Now I can just write. Whereupon I, who had three brothers and no sisters and was destined to lose my first daughter in infancy, began to write about a little girl.

I did not realise then that I was trying to manufacture the sister which I did not have and the daughter which I was to lose, though the former might have been apparent from the fact that Caddy had three brothers almost before I wrote her name on paper. I just began to write about a brother and a sister splashing one another in the brook and the sister fell and wet her clothing and the smallest brother cried, thinking that the sister was conquered or perhaps hurt. Or perhaps he knew that he was the baby and that she would quit whatever water battles to comfort him. When she did so, when she quit the water fight and stooped in her wet garments above him, the entire story, which is all told by that same little brother in the first section, seemed to explode on the paper before me.

I saw that peaceful glinting of that branch was to become the dark, harsh flowing of time sweeping her to where she could not return to comfort him, but that just separation, division, would not be enough, not far enough. It must sweep her into dishonor and shame too. And that Benjy must never grow beyond this moment; that for him all knowing must begin and end with that fierce, panting, paused and stooping wet figure which smelled like trees. That he must never grow up to where the grief of bereavement could be leavened with understanding and hence the alleviation of rage as in the case of Jason, and of oblivion as in the case of Quentin.

I saw that they had been sent to the pasture to spend the afternoon to get them away from the house during the grandmother's funeral in order that the three brothers and the nigger children could look up at the muddy seat of Caddy's drawers as she climbed the tree to look in the window at the funeral, without then realising the symbology of the soiled drawers, for here again hers was the courage which was to face later with honor the shame which she was to engender, which Quentin and Jason could not face: the one taking refuge in suicide, the other in vindictive rage which drove him to rob his bastard niece of the meagre sums which Caddy could send her. For I had already gone on to night and the bedroom and Dilsey with the mudstained drawers scrubbing the naked backside of that doomed little girl——trying to cleanse with the sorry byblow of its soiling that body, flesh, whose shame they symbolised and prophesied, as though she already saw the dark future and the part she was to play in it trying to hold that crumbling household together.

Then the story was complete, finished. There was Dilsey to be the future, to stand above the fallen ruins of the family like a ruined chimney, gaunt, patient and indomitable; and Benjy to be the past. He had to be an idiot so that, like Dilsey, he could be impervious to the future, though unlike her by refusing to accept it at all. Without thought or comprehension; shapeless, neuter, like something eyeless and voiceless which might have lived, existed merely because of its ability to suffer, in the beginning of life; half fluid, groping: a pallid and helpless mass of all mindless agony under sun, in time yet not of it save that he could nightly carry with him that fierce, courageous being who was to him but a touch and a sound that may be heard on any golf links and a smell like trees, into the slow bright shapes of sleep.

The story is all there, in the first section as Benjy told it. I did not try deliberately to make it obscure; when I realised that the story might be printed, I took three more sections, all longer than Benjy's, to try to clarify it. But when I wrote Benjy's section, I was not writing it to be printed. If I were to do it over now I would do it differently, because the writing of it as it now stands taught me both how to write and how to read, and even more: It taught me what I had already read, because on completing it I discovered, in a series of repercussions like summer thunder, the Flauberts and Conrads and Turgenievs which as much as ten years before I had consumed whole and without assimilating at all, as a moth or a goat might. I have read nothing since; I have not had to. And I have learned but one thing since about writing. That is, that the emotion definite and physical and yet nebulous to describe which the writing of Benjy's section of *The Sound and The Fury* gave me ——that ecstasy, that eager and joyous faith and anticipation of surprise which the yet unmarred sheets beneath my hand held inviolate and unfailing——will not return. The unreluctance to begin, the cold satisfaction in work well and arduously done, is there and will continue to be there as long as I can do it well. But that other will not return. I shall never know it again.

So I wrote Quentin's and Jason's sections, trying to clarify Benjy's. But I saw that I was merely temporising; That I should have to get completely out of the book. I realised that there would be compensations, that in a sense I could then give a final turn to the screw and extract some ultimate distillation. Yet it took me better than a month to take pen and write *The day dawned bleak and chill* before I did so. There is a story somewhere about an old Roman who kept at his bedside a Tyrrhenian vase which he loved and the rim of which he wore slowly away with kissing it. I had made myself a vase, but I suppose I knew all the time that I could not live forever inside of it, that perhaps to have it so that I too could lie in bed and look at it would be better; surely so when that day should come when not only the ecstasy of writing would be gone, but the unreluctance and the something worth saying too. It's fine to think that you will leave something behind you when you die, but it's better to have made something you can die with. Much better the muddy bottom of a little doomed girl climbing a blooming pear tree in April to look in the window at the funeral.

Oxford.
    19 August, 1933.

A Note on *A Fable*

[*Faulkner wrote this statement concerning* A Fable *in response to a request by his editor, Saxe Commins, late in 1953 or early in 1954, during or just after the process of editing the novel. Commins showed it to me in 1957, and I understood from him then that it had not been written as a formal preface or introduction, but had been intended as dust jacket copy, or possibly as a separate statement by the author that could be used in the pre-publication publicity for the book.*

Commins told me that he had disagreed with what Faulkner said in the statement, and had decided not to use it. And when A Fable *was published, in August 1954, the dust jacket carried on the inside back flap a very different description of the novel, which was almost certainly written by Commins. It did, however, make use of one point from Faulkner's statement, in referring briefly to "the embodiment of the trinity of man's conscience in the persons of the young aviator, the old Quartermaster General and the dedicated soldier from the ranks."—J. B. M.*]

This is not a pacifist book. On the contrary, this writer holds almost as short a brief for pacifism as for war itself, for the reason that pacifism does not work, cannot cope with the forces which produce the wars. In fact, if this book had any aim or moral (which it did not have, I mean deliberately, in its conception, since as far as I knew or intended, it was simply an attempt to show man, human beings, in conflict with their own hearts and compulsions and beliefs and the hard and durable insentient earth-stage on which their griefs and hopes must anguish), it was to show by poetic analogy, allegory, that pacifism does not work; that to put an end to war, man must either find or invent something more powerful than war and man's aptitude for belligerence and his thirst for power at any cost, or use the fire itself to fight and destroy the fire with; that man may finally have to mobilize himself and arm himself with the implements of war to put an end to war; that the mistake we have consistently made is setting nation against nation or political ideology against ideology to stop war; that the men who do not want war may have to arm themselves as for war, and defeat by the methods of war the alliances of power which hold to the obsolete belief in the validity of war: who (the above alliances) must be taught to abhor war not for moral or economic reasons, or even for simple shame, but because they are afraid of it, dare not risk it since they know that in war they themselves—not as nations or governments or ideologies, but as simple human beings vulnerable to death and injury——will be the first to be destroyed.

Three of these characters represent the trinity of man's conscience——Levine, the young English pilot, who symbolizes the nihilistic third; the old French Quartermaster general, who symbolizes the passive third; the British battalion runner, who symbolizes the active third——Levine, who sees evil and refuses to accept it by destroying himself; who says 'Between nothing and evil, I will take nothing;' who in effect, to destroy evil, destroys the world too, i.e., the world which is his, himself—— the old Quartermaster General who says in the last scene, 'I am not laughing. What you see are tears;' i.e., there is evil in the world; I will bear both, the evil and the world too, and grieve for them——the battalion runner, the living scar, who in the last scene says, 'That's right; tremble. I'm not going to die—— never.' i.e., there is evil in the world and I'm going to do something about it.

Faulkner's Speech of Acceptance for the Andres Bello Award: Caracas, 1961

[*On April 6, 1961, in Caracas, William Faulkner received from the Venezuelan government the Order of Andres Bello, first class. He made his speech of acceptance in Spanish. It was published in the Caracas newspaper* El Universal *April 7, 1961, p. 5, and that text is reprinted here.*

Faulkner's original English version has apparently disappeared, and who translated it into Spanish is not known. However, at a later date Miss Muna Lee, a Foreign Service officer who was also a poet, made a translation back into English, which is given here.——J. B. M.]

El artista, quiéralo o no, descubre con el tiempo que ha llegado a dedicarse a seguir un solo camino, un solo objetivo, del cual no puede desviarse. Esto es: tiene que tratar por todos los medios y con todo el talento que tenga—su imaginación, su propia experiencia y sus poderes de observación—poner en una forma más duradera que su instante de vida frágil y efímero— en la pintura, la escultura, la música o en un libro—lo que él ha experimentado durante un breve periodo de existencia: la pasión y la esperanza, lo bello, lo trágico, lo cómico del hombre débil y frágil, pero a la vez indómito; del hombre que lucha y sufre y triunfa en medio de los conflictos del corazón humano, de la condición humana. A él no le toca solucionar la disyuntiva ni espera sobrevivirla excepto en la forma y el significado - y las memorias que representan e invocan - del mármol, la tela, la música y las palabras ordenadas que, algún día, tendrá que dejar como su testimonio.

Esta es, sin duda, su inmortalidad, tal vez la única que le sea concedida. Quizás el mismo impulso que le condujera a esa dedicación, no era más que el simple deseo de dejar grabadas en la puerta del olvido, por la cual todos tenemos que pasar algún día, las palabras: "Lalo estuvo aqui."

Así pues, estando yo aquí, en este día de hoy, siento como si hubiara ya tocado esa inmortalidad. Porque yo, un extraño aldeano que seguía, en un lugar muy distante, esa dedicación, ese afán de intentar capturar y fijar el medio de las complejidades de su corazón, he recibido aquí, en Venezuela, la acolada que dice, en esencia: "Su dedicación no fué en vano. Lo que buscaba y encontró e intentó capturar fué la verdad."

The artist, whether or not he wishes it, discovers with the passage of time that he has come to pursue a single path, a single objective, from which he cannot deviate. That is, he must strive with all the means and all the talents he possesses—his imagination, his experience, his powers of observation—to put into more lasting form than his own frail, ephemeral instant of life—in painting, sculpture, music, or in a book—what he has known at firsthand during his brief period of existence: the passion and the hope, the beauty, the tragedy, the comedy of man, weak and frail but unconquerable; man who struggles and suffers and triumphs amid the conflicts of the human heart, the human condition. It is not his to resolve the contention nor expect to survive it, except in the form and meaning—and the memories they represent and evoke—of marble, canvas, music, and the ordered words which some day he must leave as his testament.

This undoubtedly is his immortality; it may be, the only immortality that will be granted him. Perhaps the very impulse which led him to that dedication was nothing more than the single desire to leave carved upon the portal of forgetfulness through which all of us must some day pass, the words "He passed this way."

Thus it is that I, being here today, feel as if I had already touched upon that immortality. Because I, a foreigner from a small town, who followed in a place far from here that dedication, that aspiration, striving to capture and thus fix for a moment on some pages the truth of man's hope amidst the complexities of his heart, have received here in Venezuela the accolade which says in essence: "What he sought and found and tried to capture was Truth."